Manchest

─ IN THE DAYS OF ─

STEAM

One of Aintree's large stud of 'Austin Sevens', Class 7F 0-8-0 No **49524** makes a fine sight rattling over the level crossing at Clayton Bridge with mixed freight from the Liverpool area bound, initially, for a sorting siding in the West Riding of Yorkshire. These powerful, yet temperamental locos were prone to mechanical failure, often running hot whilst working over longer distances such as this. Introduced by Fowler in 1929 as a development of the earlier LNWR G2 locos, the class originally numbered 175 but less than half remained in service at the time of the photograph. This train nicely illustrates the great variety of freight carried over the British Railways network during the 1950's. Very often, a series of short transfers at either end of a much longer journey were necessary to get goods from point A to B. When one considers that each wagon may have originated at and be bound for its own destination, it was little wonder that the whole operation could take many days to transact. More relaxed time constraints were an accepted way of commercial life in those days.

MARCH 1951 ● ARTHUR BENDELL

PAUL SHACKCLOTH

Manchester
—— IN THE DAYS OF ——
STEAM

First published 2003

ISBN 0-9543128-1-3

Published by Steam Image, PO Box 90, Cheadle Hulme, Cheshire SK8 6WZ and printed by Deanprint Ltd, Stockport, Cheshire SK3 0PR

FOREWORD

The history of railways within the City of Manchester has been well documented and, in common with the previous book published by *Steam Image*, this volume, which contains a diverse collection of photographs, is intended to complement existing works. Many of the captions have a topographical flavour which, I feel, adds an extra dimension to the scenes of yesteryear. Part One concentrates on Victoria Station and the North East Suburbs - with a special emphasis on Victoria and its environs. Opening on 1st January 1844 and named by kind permission of Her Majesty the Queen, it was the largest station in the country at the time. A part of the premises also became the headquarters of the 'Lancashire and Yorkshire Railway' - the 'business' line, as it was so often referred to. As a consequence, the complex of lines in the area are of former L&Y ownership and dominate this book's content. Included are the route to Miles Platting up the notorious incline and onwards to Droylsden via Philips Park and Clayton Bridge; the 'Manchester Loop' to Thorpes Bridge Junction, extending up the Calder Valley line to Middleton Junction, and finally the electrified line to Bury as far as Crumpsall.

ACKNOWLEDGEMENTS

Not only was the Manchester area rich in railway variety, so, fortunately, it proved to be with local cameramen. A great number of photographic sources are contained within this book - far too many to mention individually. To all who have contributed, I am eternally grateful. Certain photographs, however, remain anonymous through lack of identification. In these cases, the collector has been credited and if I have failed to acknowledge a source, please accept my sincere apology. 'Manchester in the Days of Steam' has been represented by, amongst others, H.C. Casserley, E.R. Morten, Brian Green, Graham Whitehead, Jim Davenport (courtesy of B.K.B. Green), Tom Fletcher and Richard Greenwood. The images of the late Arthur Bendell also feature prominently in this volume and I would like to thank Jeff Wells for making this material available.

Certain individuals have been instrumental in the production of this work. Trevor Moseley, John Ryan, Richard Greenwood, John Hartshorne, Fred Consterdine and Alan Gilbert were all providers of much information, giving freely of their time in both answering my questions as well as checking the detail - and all enjoyed reminiscing! In addition, Brian Green has been a constant source of encouragement - as has that other local eminent photographer, Gordon Coltas.

Once again I have integrated scenes of the major bus operators in the area and in this connection I would like to thank Peter Thompson for submitting not only his own work, but also that of Ray Dunning, which appears with the kind permission of Betty Dunning. In a similar vein, Jean Bentley has again allowed me to make use of her husband Eric's material.

Others who have contributed in one way or another include Peter Hutchinson, John Morten, Jeremy Suter, Joe Leighton, Charlie Conn, John McCracken, Paul Jordan, Richard Cort, Bob Miller, Dave Bradbury, Ken Royle, Jim Peden, David Harrop, Richard Casserley, Neville Fields, The Crich Tramway Museum, The Omnibus Society, Manchester Central Library and members of the Manchester Locomotive and Lancashire and Yorkshire Societies. Thanks also to my family, especially my wife Norma for tolerating more inconvenience and finally a special vote of thanks must be reserved for David Young and Arthur Haynes - both of whom have closely assisted me from the outset and have made many constructive comments.

An extra acknowledgement is also extended to Bernard Crick. Again he offered tireless support and, as a bonus, his knowledge of the local social and economic history proved invaluable. This is an interesting subject matter in its own right and will form the basis of future works in due course. In addition to his own excellent material, Bernard has opened up the collections of long time friends Paul Jordan, Eric Humphrey and Jeff Clough. Their work, in addition to that of another old friend, Peter Fitton, has considerably enriched the content of this work.

AUGUST 2003 ● PAUL SHACKCLOTH

DEDICATION

I wish to dedicate this book to my mother, Elsie Shackcloth. She always managed to find the five shillings which allowed her son the luxury of a day's trainspotting at Crewe. The bus fare from Moston, Nuthurst Road, to Piccadilly on services 80/88 or 112/3 was 6d each way. The return train fare was 3/6d, leaving just enough change for a couple of 1d Arrow bars and a frozen Jubbly. Happy days.

At the turn of the century, Victoria claimed to be the largest station outside London and was the headquarters of the Lancashire and Yorkshire Railway - indeed the hub of the system. After another phase of rebuilding in 1903, the original Platform 5 became Platform 11 with the introduction of a further 6 bays to cope with an ever increasing number of commuter trains serving the northern suburbs and local towns. Platform 11 usually handled the through express traffic from Yorkshire to Liverpool as well as secondary services to Bolton, Wigan and Southport. The Barton Wright 4-4-0 appears to have at least one horsebox behind the tender - a relatively common sight at the time. Three railwaymen stand by the footplate talking to the driver, whose cab is illuminated from the firebox door. On departure he would be immediately faced with a sharp double curve crossing the through LNWR roads. Three younger platelayers also get in on the act, posing for the camera in the immediate foreground. With no 'Wallside Pilot' loco in residence, the light nicely filters through the overall roof which was removed in 1935.

c.1904 ● T.T. SUTCLIFFE

This ancient engine is a 2-4-0 tender example, No 731, built by Ramsbottom at Crewe but sold when new to the East Lancs Division of the L&YR in 1873, becoming No 131. The loco was appropriated by the Chief Mechanical Engineer in 1912 and was coupled to a distinctive coupé. Although based at Horwich, she was a common sight here, often being stabled whilst the CME, Mr George Hughes, attended meetings at the Hunts Bank company headquarters. The Carriage Works at Newton Heath, the docks at Fleetwood and Goole as well as the electric line headquarters at Formby, Liverpool, were also frequently visited. No 731 received a new boiler in 1914 and survived the Grouping but was withdrawn in July 1926 after being numbered No 10000 by the LMS two years previously.

c.1913 ● PAUL SHACKCLOTH COLLECTION

Platform 12 looking in an easterly direction. A temporary halt to the busy proceedings is observed by both passengers and station staff alike, who respect the photographer's wishes, having positioned his tripod to record the scene. A porter is in the midst of loading a wicker basket on to a trolley which may well have been deposited by the overhead parcels carrier - the track is directly above. An interesting observation is the fact that every person within the scene is wearing a hat of some sort - a fashion of the Victorian period. This was the spot that many will fondly associate with trips to the seaside, as most of the departing Blackpool traffic went from here, including the prestigious 'Club' trains.

c.1900 ● PAUL SHACKCLOTH COLLECTION

The Railway, Stations and many of the Signalboxes within the North East Suburbs of Manchester (c.1950)

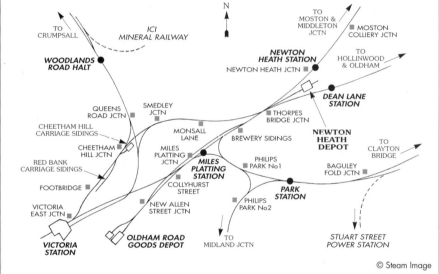

© Steam Image

One of the consequences of a rapidly expanding station was the development of parcels traffic and the acute congestion on the platforms. This prompted the Chief Mechanical Engineer, Mr. J. Aspinall, to design an ingenious overhead carrying system which he duly patented in 1895. The contract was awarded to Mather and Platt of Salford Iron Works and completed in 1899. The telpher - an electrically powered motor carriage - ran on a 300 yard circuit of track which extended the width of the station suspended from the roof. The operator controlled forward and backward movement as well as the raising and lowering of a wicker basket capable of holding up to 12 cwt of luggage. It primarily connected an elevated parcels 'station' above Platform 16 adjacent to the main Parcels Office with Platforms 11 - 1. The other station platforms tended to make use of manual labour, ie: conventional trucks supported by hoists to the luggage bridge but were supported by the carrier. The view of the recently installed system overlooks the New Bridge Street entrance at a time when the station was 'open'. The stop blocks in Platform 17 are also evident. The operator, perched high in his seat, worked an eight hour shift - not the easiest of jobs, especially during the depths of winter. The unique parcels carrier became a victim of the blitz of December 24th 1940 when the Parcels Office and much of the west end of the station roof was destroyed, completely obliterating this scene.

c.1900 ● JOHN RYAN COLLECTION

THE DREADNOUGHTS

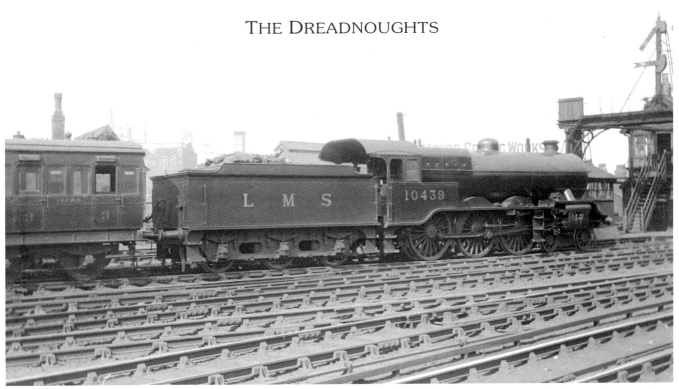

In 1908 George Hughes introduced his largest locomotives to date to cater for the ever increasing loads over the Lancashire and Yorkshire system. They were four-cylinder 4-6-0s built at Horwich and numbered 1506 - 1525 (a class of 20 engines). A batch of six, Nos 1513 - 1518, started life at Newton Heath and worked regularly to the Fylde coast, Southport and Bradford for a three year period before being transferred away for less arduous duties. Hughes's 'flagship' engine had proved to be sluggish and ineffective in service. Major modifications were necessary but the advent of the Great War postponed such activities. By 1921, however, all but five of the class had been extensively rebuilt. The transformation was immediately apparent. The superheated versions became efficient revenue earning machines and lasted for many years. As a consequence, four locos, Nos 1517/18/20 and 24, were re-allocated to Newton Heath and sent to work on the original diagrams. One of the modified locos built during the early LMS period in May 1923, No **10439** eases empty stock out of the station, signalled for the Manchester Loop line.   **JULY 1931** ● **E.R. MORTEN**

The concentration of lines at the east end of the station resulted in a multitude of semaphore signals being mounted on gantries owing to restricted clearances. Hughes 4-6-0 No **10412** draws into Platform 11 with a train from Leeds and is passing under signals controlled by the 85-lever East Junction box in view. The adjacent gantry, showing a lower quadrant off for a departure from Platform 9, was the responsibility of Turntable box which controlled all movements in and around the bays.   **JULY 1931** ● **E.R. MORTEN**

One of the later batch of modified Hughes 4-6-0's, fitted with superheaters and Walschaerts valve gear, blows off impatiently whilst standing in Platform 11. No **10456** never carried L&Y numbers, being constructed during the early LMS period at Horwich in 1924. Two years later she was converted to a 4-cylinder compound and then worked successfully on the ex-LNWR main line between Crewe and Carlisle. She returned home to the Central Division in latter years before withdrawal in March 1936. **c.1934 ● JOHN RYAN COLLECTION**

Prior to Nationalisation in January 1948, the seven surviving 'Dreadnoughts' were concentrated at Blackpool Depot. Only one, No **50455** actually received a BR number although four of the others were officially earmarked (Nos 50412/32/42 & 48). The Hughes Class 5P 4-6-0 is about to leave Victoria with the well documented 'Last of Class' excursion from Blackpool to York and return. Although she had been through Horwich Works for an 'intermediate' prior to the big day out, all was not well and Harry Woods, Chief Loco Inspector on the Central Division accompanied the Blackpool crew throughout. As predicted, problems were encountered en-route when she began knocking badly and running hot, resulting in delays to the schedule. Upon return No 50455 went into storage and was withdrawn three months later. **1st JULY 1951 ● R.S. GREENWOOD COLLECTION**

THE PEACOCKS

By the end of 1886, an acute shortage of motive power to handle the ever increasing volume of traffic left Chief Mechanical Engineer J. Aspinall with a problem. He placed an order with Beyer Peacock for thirty 4-4-0's with 6ft driving wheels which were all in service by early 1889. Popularly known as the 'Peacocks', they were based on an earlier Barton Wright design with a number of C.M.E. modifications. This example, No **997,** pictured awaiting departure from the West end platforms, worked out of Blackpool for many years.

7th JUNE 1926 ● H.C. CASSERLEY

THE '1093' 4-4-0's

The Aspinall 7' 3" 4-4-0 class were considered an intermediate size loco - larger than the 'Peacocks' yet smaller than the 'Atlantics'. No **1094**, introduced in March 1891, is seen here passing on the through road in the Agecroft direction. In June 1912 it was one of four of the original delivery to be rebuilt with Belpaire non-superheater boiler. All 40 members of the class passed into LMS control but they were extinct by 1930.

c.1913 ● PAUL SHACKCLOTH COLLECTION

L&Y 2-4-2T No 1384, fitted with Belpaire boiler, awaits departure from the station. A local instruction to all enginemen within the immediate vicinity of Victoria was to keep smoke emission to an absolute minimum. The dirty chimney observed here would hopefully soon be under control. The combined exhausts, especially during the morning rush hour, often created a perpetual gloom which lasted all day. Trains starting out from neighbouring Exchange Station and passing through the middle roads in the days when the overall roof was in-situ, must have only compounded the problem.

7th JUNE 1926 ● H.C. CASSERLEY

The sheer volume of medium and short distance passenger trains over the ex-L&Y system was reflected in the number of these 2-4-2 side tank engines designed by Aspinall. 330 locomotives were spread over the network - by far the largest number of this type at work in Great Britain. Various modifications were made over the years and this particular loco, No **10912** (L&Y No 253), was originally one of a handful in the final series to be given express link status. By the LMS period she was engaged on more sedate duties - for example this all stations from Normanton train.

JULY 1931 ● **E.R. MORTEN**

THE 2-4-2 TANKS

An unidentified member awaits the signal away from Platform 13. The front numberplate had been removed, which was not unusual, and the loco is sporting a 23D Wigan (L&Y) shedplate. Nearly one third of the class survived into the BR period, some of which had been in service for nearly 60 years - a testament to their durability.

c.1936 ● **PAUL SHACKCLOTH COLLECTION**

One of the original 2-4-2's with short bunkers, L&Y '1008' Class No **1039**, drifts through the platforms light engine on her way to Agecroft shed. She became LMS No 10636 at the grouping and BR No 50636 at Nationalisation before being finally withdrawn from Manningham in July 1957.

7th JUNE 1926 ● **H.C. CASSERLEY**

An early Atlantic 4-4-2 No 1393 is about to depart for home from Platform 13 with the 8.20am express to Leeds. The loco had arrived earlier in the morning on the 3.20am mail train. These engines made a spectacular introduction when unveiled by Aspinall in 1899. 40 were built in two groups and the high pitched boiler made for an ungainly appearance. Renowned for their hard work and reliability, these mighty engines, nicknamed 'Highflyers', were the mainstay class for express passenger workings over the L&Y for many years, substituting on many occasions for the more powerful, yet occasionally unreliable 'Dreadnought' locos.   **c.1910 ● A. HAYNES COLLECTION**

THE 'HIGHFLYERS'

Sister loco No 718 stands awaiting return to its native Liverpool. The shed serving the Exchange terminus - Sandhills - was the L&Y's main passenger depot whilst Aintree handled the bulk of freight traffic. Sandhills became known as Bank Hall after 1920, at which time the depot became a 'running department' or head depot, with Aintree, Southport and Ormskirk acting as sub-sheds. It was coded 18 and No 718 would display that number on a small enamel sign within the cab roof.

c.1910 ● A. HAYNES COLLECTION

THE BALTIC TANKS

The ten 4-6-4 Baltic Tanks that Hughes constructed at Horwich were the last genuine L&Y locos - although they were introduced shortly after the Grouping in 1924. These huge machines were a development of the 'Dreadnoughts' but were considered unsuitable for many Central Lines duties. A pair were tried between Bedford and St. Pancras whilst three members worked between London Road and Buxton for some time. After other trials they gravitated to Agecroft and Bolton to serve out their time. No **11114,** standing in Platform 16, has its train heating pipe disconnected - perhaps a sign of summer. This particular loco appeared in the 1925 Wembley exhibition and was one of a trio painted in standard LMS red.

c.1938 ● R.S. GREENWOOD COLLECTION

LANKY 'A' CLASS

Although classed as a freight locomotive the Lanky 'A' 0-6-0's were frequently employed on stopping passenger work in both the L&Y & LMS periods. They also saw extensive service on various relief and excursion trains in BR days during the 1950's, especially during the 'Wakes Week' periods. Many a locomotive was serviced at either Blackpool North or Central Depot after helping deliver a significant proportion of a town's population to the traditional holiday resort. No **12264** brings a stopping train from Normanton into the station off the Manchester 'Loop' line.

JULY 1931 ● **E. R. MORTEN**

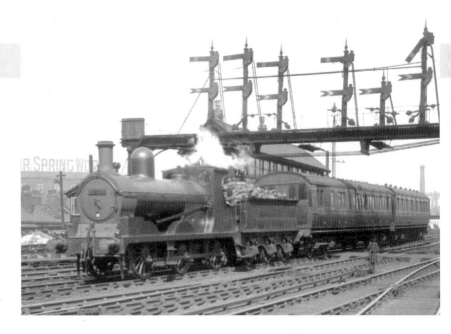

Perhaps the most common sight at Manchester Victoria Station over the years was a pair of ex-L&Y Aspinall 0-6-0's on the 'Wallside Pilot' duty. The first examples were introduced in 1889 and nearly 500 were eventually built over a 30 year period with minor design variations. During both L&Y and LMS periods, Newton Heath had large numbers on its allocation and even in early BR days (1950) still had 20 members to call on. They were specifically detailed to assist traffic climbing the notorious Miles Platting Incline (1 in 59/47) as well as trains up the Cheetham Hill Loop. Nos **52207** and **52094** await their next turns of duty. The smaller of the two station buffets was situated on Platform 12 (behind No 52094) and during the quieter moments it offered locomen a convenient facility to top up their billy cans. **1952** ● **R.S. CARPENTER**

The last in the line. When No **52271** moved 'up the road' to Lees, Oldham in April 1961, it ended not only Newton Heath Depot's 72 year old association with the class, but with all ex-L&Y locomotives. The Class 3F 0-6-0s had found continuous employment on Manchester Victoria's various pilot duties for nigh on 72 years. With the calling-on signal in its favour, No 52271 cautiously approaches the brake van to offer assistance.

JULY 1960 ● **J. DAVENPORT**

A rare photo of the original Irwell Bridge Sidings signalbox situated above the river on the border of the Cities of Manchester and Salford. Built in 1895, it had 28 levers and controlled, amongst other things, the spur on which a member of the Aspinall 7' 3" 4-4-0 family is standing. This is the spot where either no 344 or 430, both of which were kept in immaculate condition by Newton Heath, spent many years acting as 'West End Pilot' with regular drivers. On this occasion, however, the loco is carrying a headboard letter 'B' on the smokebox door, signifying an impending trip to Blackpool Central. This was a Summer seasonal destination indicator, the letter 'A' indicating Blackpool Talbot Road. It may well be waiting to relieve an ailing loco on a through working.   **c.1912 ● A. HAYNES COLLECTION**

Sunlight streams through the overall roof covering the west end of platforms 12 to 17. It was this section which was subjected to heavy bombardment during the wartime blitz, removed by the Luftwaffe and never replaced. The conditions also show off the elegant lines of Barton Wright 4-4-0 No **842** standing in Platform 12. She entered service in May 1884 as one of a large family, being built by Neilson - one of a number of outside contractors employed by Barton Wright. 10 members of the 110 strong class originally carried nameplates but these were soon removed for obscure reasons. They were short lived and only two survived into the LMS period being replaced by more powerful locos under Aspinall's direction. No 842 was one of the first to go - as early as November 1904.   **c.1902 ● R.S. GREENWOOD COLLECTION**

STATION APPROACHES

The only bus service running directly to the station in recent years had been the No 109 from Reddish, Houldsworth Square. A brand new Leyland Atlantean Mancunian No **1005** (HVM 905F), working out of Hyde Road Garage, is on the new No 19 service, part of a renumbering scheme which preceded the introduction of these vehicles on 1st April 1968 amidst much publicity. At this time the No 19 route in Reddish was cut back to Bull's Head to keep the route inside the Manchester City Transport operating area, within which a simplified fare structure had been introduced (note the 'coin-in-the-slot' signs above the windscreen) to facilitate driver-only operation.
17th APRIL 1968 ● PAUL SHACKCLOTH COLLECTION

The original station dating back to 1844 is to the left of the main building at the top of Hunts Bank approach with the popular Grill Room occupying the ground floor at this point. Equally imposing on the right is the L&Y's former parcels office building. When new facilities were developed on the north side of the station, Hunts Bank Central Division Control took over a part of the ground floor whilst other rooms were converted for officers and agents of the railway. Demolition came about ten years after the end of steam, at which time the soot-ridden station facade, designed by William Davies and eventually completed in 1909, was given a much needed facelift. The architectural splendour of Victoria and the neighbouring Chethams College was now there for all to admire.
17th APRIL 1954 ● H.C. CASSERLEY

The imposing station facade contained Company offices and featured a long, glazed canopy covering the pavement as far as the verandah. The roof incorporated destinations served from Manchester including those abroad by way of the L&YR's ferry services. A large tiled map of the system and official memorial unveiled by Earl Haig in 1922 lie within one of three main entrances into the station concourse. The verandah spanning Victoria Station Approach was rendered unsafe and promptly demolished after falling victim to a Sheffield JOC bus which struck a supporting column. The service between Sheffield and Manchester, via Stocksbridge and Woodhead, started in October 1929. It was classed as a 'C' service, whereby the buses were owned by the LMS or LNE railways, but operated by Sheffield Corporation under the auspices of the Sheffield Joint Omnibus Committee. In May 1937, Sheffield bus No 183, a Leyland TS7 single-deck with Cravens bodywork, skidded and caused spectacular damage. The bus carried the emblem of the LMS railway on the bodyside, as the service (later better known as the 48) started from the former LMS station in Sheffield and terminated at Victoria Station. Shortly after 1950 this was moved to Exchange Station.   **c.1912 ● JOHN RYAN COLLECTION**

The most popular approach from the heart of the city was off Corporation Street by way of Todd Street. This familiar view, encountered by millions of passengers over many years, shows the south corner of the building which features the legend 'Lancashire and Yorkshire Railway' beneath the clock within the stonework. A fourth entrance, that off Long Millgate is tucked away behind 'Nellies fruiterer and florist' canopy. This was commonly known as 'Cigar Alley', the reasons for which remain obscure. One theory is that 'Dunhills' products were sold from a kiosk just within this end of the concourse. The Victoria Club on the opposite corner had a seedy reputation. Apparently the purchase of a hot pie and baked beans, served on a cardboard plate, entitled the customer to make use of the bar outside the normal licensing hours!   **29th JULY 1966 ● H.C. CASSERLEY**

The view from within the concourse.
17th APRIL 1967 ● BERNARD CRICK

The Millgate entrance was opposite the short Halliwell Street which, in turn, led to Corporation Street. The days of steam were also the days of unrestricted parking on side streets such as this within the city. To the right stood the fish dock which was walled off from the bay platforms. A train arrived here every weekday at 9.00am from Aberdeen *(Mondays excepted)* after having passed through Victoria Middle as far as Millgate Signalbox and setting back. The bay was demolished at the same time as the Hunts Bank offices in 1978.   29th JUNE 1968 ● DAVE JESSOP

The view looking down the concourse from the Millgate entrance. The Booking, Enquiry and Left Luggage Offices are signed to the left whilst the distinctive Refreshment Room with domed roof is straight ahead. The first of two W.H. Smith & Son bookstalls is prominent, situated behind the stop blocks of Platforms 4 and 5. This is where many Manchester trainspotters bought their Ian Allan 'ABC's and monthly editions of 'Trains Illustrated'. This particular stall is happily preserved and functioning as such at the Severn Valley Railway's Kidderminster Station. The second bookstall is at the far end of the concourse, beyond the Information Bureau and near the barrier to Platforms 11 - 17. The trolley in the foreground is loaded with cartons containing 'Maltesers' and the ever popular 'Mars Bar'.

1955 ● STATIONS UK

Looking down the platform from just inside the ticket barrier which allowed access on and off Nos 1 and 2. In latter days, the former handled arrivals from Bury on the intensive electric service and No 2 the departures although not exclusively so. A quiet spell exposes the presence of vans and a flat wagon over in the other bays. The luggage bridge spanning the station and the hydraulic lifts to platform level are prominent beyond which Cheetham Hill Road bridge catches the midday sun. The clattering of the mechanical train indicators, an example of which is seen here, will strike a happy chord with many older commuters.

1955 ● STATIONS UK

CORPORATION STREET

A busy Corporation Street looking towards Victoria Station. Leyland Titan PD1/3 No **3092** (GVR 294) waits for the lights by Trevelyan Buildings at Cannon Street before crossing the city on the No 75, Heaton Park to Greenheys, Platt Lane service. An unidentified Daimler CVG6 follows on the No 81 service from Hightown to Southern Cemetery. Both routes were shared between Queens and Princess Road Garages. Leyland PD2/3 No **3219** (JND 620) heads north out of town with an extra to Middleton, the No 17X service. A Triumph Mayflower overtakes whilst behind the Daimler is a rag and bone cart piled high after rich pickings in the Cheetham district. Kemsley House on the corner of Withy Grove is prominent and was home to, amongst others, the *Daily Dispatch* and the *Evening Chronicle* - which became part of the *Manchester Evening News* in 1962. In those days both football and Rugby League supporters had the choice of Green or Pink Finals to choose from. There was a keen rivalry to be first off the press on a Saturday evening ready for supporters returning to the city after the game at either Maine Road, Old Trafford, Station Road or The Willows.   **c1956 ● A.D. PACKER**

VICTORIA STREET

Bogie car No 924 is bound for Stockport, Mersey Square with a shortened 35 service. She was one of a series built by the Car Works at Hyde Road and completed in late 1921 but a national economic depression dictated that she did not start work until March 1922. Nos 35 & 35C were the last remaining tram services operated by Manchester Corporation, ceasing running on 9th January 1949 and transferring to bus operation the following day. The 35 originally ran from Albert Square to Hazel Grove but was re-routed down Market Street to its new Exchange terminus in April 1925. Replacement bus service No 92, now running between Piccadilly and Hazel Grove, remained jointly operated with Stockport Corporation. Birchfields Road depot provided new Crossleys numbered 2110 - 2151 for the purpose. Note the air raid shelter still in situ behind which is Chethams School on Fennel Street and a glimpse of the ballustraded facade of Victoria station.

c1948 ● A.D. PACKER

By June 1960 many of the suburban trains were in the hands of Diesel Multiple Units An original Cravens motor composite is in view, about to depart from Platform 7 with the 4.55pm all stations to Royton. Meanwhile Stanier Class 4 2-6-4T No **42619** waits on the stabling road between Platforms 8 and 9 before setting her stock back into No 9, forming the 5.03pm all stations to Stalybridge. Minutes later the 5.06pm to Oldham and Rochdale, the 5.11pm to Bacup and the 5.18pm, also to Oldham and Rochdale will have departed from Nos 8, 6 and 7 platforms respectively. This typified the intensity of service still witnessed at this time. Between 4.00pm and 6.00pm no fewer than 57 trains departed from all platforms. One every two minutes!   **22nd JUNE 1960 ● GRAHAM WHITEHEAD**

THE BAY PLATFORMS

During the early 1950's, steam still reigned supreme but major changes were in the air. British Railways selected the Bacup branch as one of the first lines to become dieselised as early as 1956. Derby-built lightweight two car sets, often operating in pairs were selected. The writing was on the wall for Fairburn Class 4MT 2-6-4T No **42278** awaiting departure from the seldom used No 10 platform with the 4.25pm to Stalybridge. The train called at Miles Platting, Park (Fridays and Saturdays only), Clayton Bridge, Droylsden and Ashton. Standing alongside is BR Standard Class 4MT 2-6-4T No **80049** with the 4.20pm all stations to Middleton.

c.1956 ● J. DAVENPORT

A time for quiet contemplation. A BR official leans against the wrought iron railings protecting the back of No 11 platform whilst Stanier Class Five 4-6-0 No **44818** is also at rest between duties within No 9 platform. The newly constructed CIS building towers over the station, which was built to replace the original distinctive premises just in view on the extreme left hand side beyond Cheetham Hill Road bridge. Between No 44818's chimney and dome is the Ducie Bridge Hotel, behind which is the Union Cold Storage Company on Miller Street whose premises have a water tank on the roof.

JULY 1967 ● DAVE JESSOP

Another unidentified Class Five works within the bays during the final months of steam. Part of the original glass canopied roof is still in evidence but the semaphores were replaced by colour light signals in conjunction with the opening of the new Victoria East Junction box in 1962.

MARCH 1968 ● PAUL SHACKCLOTH

Fairburn 2-6-4 Tank No 42279 moves its stock out of Platform 4 and under Cheetham Hill Road Bridge after bringing in a local train from Rochdale via the Oldham loop line.

c.1957 ● D. LAWRENCE

THE BAYS PILOTS

Three views of Stanier Class Five 4-6-0 No 44780 on Pilot duty in Platform 8.

1 - Standing within the trainshed. The poster on the concourse reveals that Blackpool Central Pier is 'now open' after having suffered the ravages of storm damage during the winter. A decade or so earlier the options available for a trip to the resort were as follows: A day excursion ticket (Departing at 9am) cost 5 shillings. A half day excursion (Lunchtime) cost 3 shillings and sixpence whilst the evening trip (5pm) cost half a crown. For an extra shilling, the ticket would also admit entrance to the Tower Ballroom (a stone's throw from Central Station) on the occasions when Reginald Dixon rose from the depths, playing his Wurlitzer organ which he did for so many years.

2 - Having drawn forward, the loco is now standing just clear of both the awning and wrought iron luggage girder bridge which ran the full width of the station. A local instruction to the footplatemen was not to come to a stand with the chimney directly underneath this bridge. The austere cladding protecting the end section of the roof covering Platforms 5-10 was supposedly a temporary measure. Although a rebuilding programme within the vicinity of Victoria and Exchange stations was tabled, economics determined that it was never to happen.

3 - The Newton Heath crew await their next instructions. By this time a surplus of this class of loco left in service would cover virtually every working. Note the angle of the timbers to the platform edge.

16TH MAY 1968 ● PAUL SHACKCLOTH

The morning parcels train from Stockport has arrived in Platform 3 behind Fowler 2-6-4T No 42357. Meanwhile the Turntable Pilot, Fowler 2-6-2T No 40013 has reversed on and will shortly remove the empty vans, allowing the Edgeley loco to be released from the stop blocks. Although Platform 3 carried the electrified third rail for the Bury services, it tended to act only as an overspill for Platforms 1 and 2. In 1959 there were departures at 7.20am, 12.00SX and 5.00pmSX. In addition, a diesel train left for Bacup at 7.05pm, calling at all stations except Miles Platting. It took the electrified route through Collyhurst Tunnel before traversing the Irk Valley Junction - Smedley Junction chord, gaining access to the Down Slow line and Thorpes Bridge Junction from where it continued the journey via Moston, Castleton South Junction, Heywood and Bury Knowsley Street.

14th OCTOBER 1959 ● R.S. GREENWOOD

A 'Breadvan' could often be found performing the Turntable Pilot duty which covered Bay Platforms No 1-10. This was considered less arduous than the other pilot work around the station and these locos were rarely seen on the 'Wallside'. Although members of the class performed sterling work on the outer London commuter services from both Euston and St Pancras, they were universally unpopular with Newton Heath men and found little regular work. Fowler Class 3MT 2-6-2T No 40063 stands on the Turntable Spur immediately beyond Cheetham Hill Road Bridge. The driver had to receive a verbal instruction to move off this short spur by the signalman at the 124 lever Turntable signalbox, a request which appeared to happen rather infrequently. In L&Y days there were no fewer than three turntables within the immediate vicinity of Victoria Station. The spur and signalbox took their names from a 50ft example which was once situated just behind the loco.

4th MAY 1960 ● IAN G. HOLT

The standard procedure for many years upon arrival by certain trains into the suburban platforms was as follows. Whilst discharging the passengers, the fireman would uncouple his loco from the leading carriage. Then, responding to the guard, who had pulled the strings to release the vacuum brake, and a clear signal, the driver would propel the empty stock beyond Cheetham Hill Road bridge to a designated point and come to a stand. The guard would apply the hand brake allowing the loco to drift back into the short spur in front of Turntable signalbox. The path would then be set for the stock to gravitate into the selected platform, once more making judicious use of the hand brake. LMS Stanier Class 4 2-6-4T No 2624 has completed such an operation and both points and calling on signal are set for the stock to gently roll into No 9 platform.

24th APRIL 1947 ● H. C. CASSERLEY

A football excursion carrying Sheffield Wednesday supporters passes through the station at 12.03pm. The F.A. Cup tie against Bolton Wanderers is at Burnden Park with a scheduled 3pm kick off, therefore the destination is Trinity Street Station. The train will have traversed the Woodhead route, departing from Sheffield Victoria around 10.30am with the Darnall B1 4-6-0 No **61311** (39B) working throughout, arriving at this point via Ashburys, Midland, Philips Park and Miles Platting Junctions. A Newton Heath pilotman is probably on the footplate assisting the Sheffield crew with the necessary route knowledge for the last leg of the journey. The commencement of electrified services on the ex-GC line between Manchester, London Road and Sheffield Victoria was still three months away. For the record, Sheffield Wednesday won the game 2-0 in front of 52,568 spectators.   **17th MARCH 1954** ⚫ **B.K.B. GREEN**

VICTORIA EAST JUNCTION

A Blackpool-bound excursion drifts into Victoria Station behind Stanier Class Five 4-6-0 No **44893.** The loco carries Central Lines reporting number C892 and has worked the non-corridor stock via Miles Platting. The train may have started out from the Oldham area travelling by way of the OA&GB route. On this occasion, the turntable pilot is a Fairburn Class 4 2-6-4T and can be glimpsed above the inevitable trainspotters hogging the end of Platform 11.   **26th SEPTEMBER 1953** ⚫ **P. HUTCHINSON**

Stanier Class Five 4-6-0 No 45290 brings empty stock into Victoria's Platform 12 to form a train bound for Fleetwood. The intensive timetable of residential traffic to both Southport and the Fylde coast resulted in a constant procession of trains from mid afternoon right through the rush hour. Queens Road and Cheetham Hill Carriage Sidings were mainly responsible for stabling the stock. Newton Heath made much use of its large stud of over 30 Class Fives for the work, augmented by its other Class 6 and 7 motive power. Blackpool bound trains tended to use Platform 12 whilst Southport workings usually went from Platform 11 or 11 middle.

6th AUGUST 1960 ● **J. DAVENPORT**

The forerunner of the class, Fowler 4-6-0 No 45500 *Patriot* eases forward with empty stock. After spending virtually all its 26 year life on the Western Division it came to the Central Division and worked out of Newton Heath for its last 12 months, being withdrawn during September 1961. The light engine drifting down the bank is Stanier Class Five 4-6-0 No **45056** from Holyhead - a comparative stranger. The shell of the new Victoria East Junction signal box stands alongside its ex-L&Y counterpart of the same name. It would be a further 18 months before it was to open in the Spring of 1962, at which time it replaced seven boxes in the immediate vicinity. They were the original East Junction, Turntable, Millgate, Newtown 1 & 2, Footbridge and Cheetham Hill Junction.   **3rd SEPTEMBER 1960** ● **B.W.L. BROOKSBANK**

The new box was fully operational when Jim Davenport recorded this scene. Ivatt Class 2 2-6-0 No **46419** rests almost within its shadows between spells of pilot duty. The old familiar signal gantry, already without its arms would shortly be demolished. Stanier Jubilee 4-6-0 No **45706** *Express* brings yet more empty non-corridor stock from Lightbowne Sidings round the loop (or New Line) and through Manchester Victoria middle. The train is destined for Swinton from where it will form an inter-regional excursion. Also recording the scene is one of the many spotters who would congregate under Cheetham Hill Road bridge at the East end of Platform 11. The 'Coronet' camera and school jacket nicely complete the picture.

4th MAY 1962 ● **J. DAVENPORT**

Another cautious descent of the bank brings a Wakefield WD 2-8-0 No **90054** through the middle with a mineral train for Ordsall Lane. By this time the class, once numbering 733 locos, had only 28 months of active service left with Stanier 8Fs and even Class Fives gradually taking over their duties. Withdrawals began in earnest from 1962 onwards until the surviving 24, all based on the North Eastern Region of BR, were condemned en-bloc in September 1967.   **3rd MARCH 1965 ● BERNARD CRICK**

The fireman returns to the cab of 'Austin Seven', Fowler 7F 0-8-0 No 49618 after having unpinned the brakes of each wagon making up his train. Footplatemen needed no reminding of their strict adherence to the rule book here, and many were conscious of an earlier disaster when a train ran away down the 2,320 yard long Miles Platting bank, resulting in tragic consequences. Lanky 'A' Class 0-6-0 No **52271**, a regular performer, is one of the 'Wallside Pilots'.   **2nd APRIL 1960 ● PETER FITTON**

In February 1958 Gorton Shed passed from Eastern Region to London Midland Region control but the works continued to handle certain classes of ex-LNER locos. One such class was the numerous Robinson 04 2-8-0. The Gorton contingent had been a familiar sight here for many years, usually working through on Ardwick - Brindle Heath transfer goods. No **63605** is a stranger in the camp though, returning eastbound on a running-in turn, but seeing a member in immaculate condition such as this was a rare sight. She had recently passed through the paint shop at the Works following a last major overhaul there. One would like to think that a 56B shedplate will be fitted to the smokebox door on the loco's return to Ardsley depot where she had been based since January 1954.

28th AUGUST 1959 ● MERCHANT NAVY LOCOMOTIVE PRESERVATION SOCIETY

Occasionally locos received 'front end jobs' while the remainder was ignored and left in typically grubby condition. Such was the case with LMS Hughes/Fowler Class 6P 5F 2-6-0 No **42750** whose bright red bufferbeam and recently painted smokebox door would have caught photographer Jim Davenport's eye well before he pressed the shutter. The rear of the mineral train is adjacent to Millgate signalbox and of further interest are the four figures featuring in the photograph, possibly staff connected with the construction of the new East Junction power box.

28th JULY 1961 ● J. DAVENPORT

By 1968 there was little or no variety of loco left in service and 'gricing' began to lose a lot of its charm. The diehards were left to record only numbers of Class Fives of Stanier and Standard variety supported by 9F's and the trusty Stanier 8F's. These were the staple diet and anything else was considered a bonus. 'Cops' by now were a rarity. No **48756** works through a deserted station with a mixed goods train. I often wondered what might have been at the head of such a train in the so called halcyon days, but perhaps more importantly, all the other activity that would have been witnessed in and around one of the country's once busiest stations.

NOVEMBER 1967 ● PAUL SHACKCLOTH

Bank Hall often provided Class Five motive power for its fast and semi-fast passenger turns to Manchester and beyond. It was unusual, however to find one on the 10-30am ex-Liverpool Exchange - Newcastle, substituting in this case for the usual Jubilee. No **44688** arrives on time in Platform 13 with the train on a bright sunny morning. The irregular shaped building was a purpose-built parcels office and stood on the corner of New Bridge Street and Ducie Street on land once occupied by a fish market. Built in 1895, provision was also made for the Passenger Superintendent's Department whose offices occupied the upper storeys, opening directly on to the west end of Platform 16.

19th APRIL 1954 ● H.C. CASSERLEY

The same train just over five years later produced this loco one damp and misty morning. The transfer in July 1958 of Fowler 4-6-0 No **45517** to Bank Hall raised a few eyebrows as the unrebuilt 'Pats' had largely been associated with the principal depots on the ex-LNWR lines. This un-named example arrived from Willesden to provide support for the shed's small stud of Jubilees. Shortly afterwards the class became more widespread as firstly Newton Heath (No 45509) then Bristol, Barrow Road (Nos 45504/6/19) received members. No 45517 became a regular performer on the 'Newcastle' for over three years although certain Bank Hall men always preferred to take a Stanier Class Five if one of their 'Jubs' wasn't available. After dieselisation of the Calder Valley services, little work remained and she was withdrawn in June 1962.

26th OCTOBER 1959 ● R. S. GREENWOOD

In the early L&Y days, Manchester Victoria was an 'open' station with booking facilities available at various locations. This was the booking office on Platforms 12 and 13, direct access to which could be gained up an incline leading from Great Ducie Street where a space for cabs was available. When open for business, passengers booked under the cover of the ill fated roof which offered protection. To cope with the heavy seasonal demand, an excursion office was also sited towards the top of this incline. Even in BR days these platforms were always considered the hub of the station, with No 12 in particular handling a great proportion of the Blackpool traffic. The station became 'closed' in March 1913 and barriers were erected. From that time all bookings and reservations were concentrated within the main concourse. The former booking office, whose windows are boarded over, was utilised by Passenger Control in later years.

8th OCTOBER 1967 ● PAUL SHACKCLOTH

Train indicator boards remained in use throughout the steam era. Familiar local destinations found on Platform 13 are discernable and one showing the longest journey from the station is of particular interest. It reads: Bolton, Preston, Lancaster, Penrith, Carlisle, Carstairs, (Front Portion Motherwell and Glasgow; rear, Edinburgh).

8th OCTOBER 1967 ● PAUL SHACKCLOTH

▶

The late afternoon sun catches long time resident Jubilee 4-6-0 No **45635** *Tobago* drifting through Victoria Station middle, light engine. The time on the station clock shows 4.45pm and the train standing in Platform 12 is one of the smartly timed residential 'Club Trains'. The 5.03pm Manchester - Blackpool, first stop Blackpool South, took just over the hour and was due to arrive in Central Station at 6.11pm. The roof covering the through platforms (12 - 16) looks impressive but this is the section that survived the extensive damage inflicted by the Luftwaffe during the night of 23rd December 1940.

8th SEPTEMBER 1960 ● PETER FITTON

Platform 12   8th OCTOBER 1967 ● PAUL SHACKCLOTH

▶

Newton Heath's Jubilees were often employed working over the ex-LNWR main line to Leeds. No **45701** *Conqueror* blasts its way through Manchester Victoria Middle and is about to attack the notorious Miles Platting incline (1 in 59/47). The train is the 2.05pm SSO Liverpool Lime Street to Newcastle and the loco will probably be relieved at Leeds City by an ex-LNER Pacific from Heaton or Gateshead, but on days such as this, a Summer Saturdays Only train could be placed in the hands of literally whatever was available. Such was the spice of trainspotting in the 1950's. One of Patricroft's large stud of Standard Class Fives drifts back down the bank and passes under Cheetham Hill Road Bridge. This loco may well be the Exchange Pilot, returning after assisting the previous departure out of Exchange Station. *Conqueror* may therefore have 'rushed the bank' unassisted. If it falters, a crow on the whistle will be the signal for one of 26A's 'Wallside Pilots' to buffer up behind.

25th JULY 1957 ● ERIC BENTLEY

Newton Heath's Jubilees

The fireman of Jubilee 4-6-0 No 45710 *Irresistible* casts a glance towards the west end shunter's cabin, situated just off Platforms 12 and 13. Judging by the amount of coal carefully trimmed on the Fowler 3,500 gallon tender, he will soon be in for a spell of hard labour! This engine/tender combination was considered far from satisfactory. Apart from the barely adequate supply of coal for the Glasgow turns, the engines were prone to rough riding and some developed injector problems. When *Irresistible* became due for heavy overhaul at Crewe Works in February 1959, the opportunity was taken of pairing it with a Stanier 4,000 gallon tender, in this case No 10328 (ex 8F No 48601). Other members of the class were treated in a similar way as they became due for shopping but a few slipped the net, remaining coupled to the Fowler version until withdrawal. The Jubilee is being piloted by an unidentified Class Five which may well be returning north off an unbalanced working. The leading coach is of interest, being an early LMS type complete with distinctive panelling. **c.1957 ● J.D. OWENS**

The lengthy through platforms at Victoria handled a considerable volume of traffic. Nos 11 and 12 dealt primarily with arrivals from the east and departures to the west whereas Nos 13 to 16 were more versatile. It was not uncommon to find two trains occupying the same platform before departing in opposite directions. Jubilee 4-6-0 No **45710 *Irresistible,*** now paired with its new tender, makes a fine sight whilst standing in Platform 14 prior to departure with the 1.30pm express to Carlisle. **25th OCTOBER 1961 ● DON CASH**

The year of 1963 saw the final months of extensive usage of the Jubilee Class at Newton Heath. Their swan song was perhaps on the morning of Good Friday, 12th April when no less than four members were observed on passenger duties at Manchester Victoria during a half hour period. Perhaps the most prestigious duty fell to No **45652 *Hawke,*** a former Midland Lines stalwart which had charge of an extra train to Glasgow Central. It is seen here making a memorably volatile start out of Platform 11 Middle and into Exchange Station on the through line. The summer timetable heralded the withdrawal of old faithfuls Nos 45701 *Conqueror*, 45702 *Colossus*, 45706 *Express* and shortly afterwards No 45710 *Irresistible*. No 45652 *Hawke* was to move on to Warrington Dallam, its final destination.   **12th APRIL 1963** ● **PAUL JORDAN**

Something of a mystery surrounds this photograph. Stanier Class 6P Jubilee 4-6-0 No **45701 *Conqueror*** is captured on 'Wallside Pilot' duties as early as 1960. At this time the work was still largely the province of the ex-L&Y 'A' Class 0-6-0's, often supported by the Ivatt 2-6-0's. One wonders if the loco was hastily commandeered into service to replace another loco. A further puzzle is *Conqueror's* condition. The front of the loco has obviously received a smokebox repaint, possibly after scorching, but precious little else appears to have been done.

8th SEPTEMBER 1960 ● **PETER FITTON**

By 1966, little work was available for the last remaining member on the books, No **45654 *Hood***. Apart from featuring on the occasional railtour, the loco was often reduced to Wallside duties. How the mighty had fallen. The fireman is Dorian Greenidge who, with others, moved from Lees (Oldham) on 5th March 1962. He is related to the former Hampshire and West Indies opening batsman Gordon Greenidge.

3rd JUNE 1966 ● **GRAHAM WHITEHEAD**

Everyday visitors to the station were Wigan (L&Y) Stanier 2-6-4 tanks working the local services from Southport and their home town. No **2554** makes use of the crossover between Platforms 13 and 14 between duties. Note the scars and starkness of scene - the results of recent wartime damage. Timbers have replaced that part of the platform which took a direct 'hit' and were to remain in-situ until eventually being swept away as part of large scale remodelling - many years after the demise of steam. At this point the loco would have been almost under the apex of the original roof which was damaged beyond repair and cut back to the surviving portion in view.   **18th OCTOBER 1946** ● H.C. CASSERLEY

LIGHT ENGINES

Out of a class numbering 842 locos, only four Stanier Class Fives (45154/6/7/8) carried nameplates and these were allocated to St Rollox (Glasgow) in the early 1950's. In April 1957 it was something of a surprise when the authorities transferred two of them south to Newton Heath. Nearly two years later, No **45156 *Ayrshire Yeomanry*** is reversing through the station still showing her large 'Scottish' cab side numerals - a practice of the ex-Caledonian workshops at St Rollox.

13th MARCH 1959 ● R.S. GREENWOOD

The Stanier 8Fs were a successful wartime locomotive and many saw service overseas before returning home. Introduced in 1935, they were designed to haul heavy freight over long distances at relatively low speeds. As a consequence, the moving parts were unbalanced. After the war their speeds were restricted to 40mph but a number of the class had their balancing improved, enabling them to run at faster speeds which then encompassed passenger work. The modified locomotives were distinguished by a star immediately below the number on the cab side. No **48716,** fitted with Fowler tender, was one such engine seen here passing through Victoria middle.

8th SEPTEMBER 1960 ● PETER FITTON

SOCIETY RAILTOURS

The Manchester and Stephenson Locomotive Societies organised many joint railtours. The 'Northern Dales' is about to leave behind ex-LMS Compound 4-4-0 No **41102** (24E - Blackpool). She worked the train as far as Tebay via Hellifield and Low Gill before being relieved. After visiting Darlington, the Fighting Cocks Branch to Eaglescliffe and thence via Northallerton and Wensleydale to Hawes, No 41102 was re-attached. Ex-LNER D20 4-4-0 No 62360 acted as pilot to Garsdale on the way home, which was via Hellifield and Blackburn.

4th SEPTEMBER 1955 ● **A. HAYNES COLLECTION**

Ten members of the 52 strong Patriot Class never carried nameplates although, in some cases, names had been earmarked. The last unrebuilt example to be honoured was No **45509** in November 1951, although the loco had been built at Crewe some nineteen years earlier. *The Derbyshire Yeomanry* was an impressive double lined brass plate and came complete with regimental crest. The naming ceremony, fittingly, took place at Derby where the loco had been transferred. It was something of a surprise when it arrived at Newton Heath in 1958 as the class were relatively uncommon on the Central Division. Apparently the ex-Midland men were glad to see the back of it and its condition on arrival left much to be desired. It was immediately booked in for a heavy general repair which it received at Crewe in 1959. With the nameplate glinting in the afternoon sun, No 45509, in ex-works condition, makes a fine sight awaiting departure. The train is the 'Northern Fells Tour' which departed at 10.10am, picking up at Bolton, Preston and Lancaster Castle before traversing the Glasson Dock branch (closed to passengers in 1930). It returned to Lancaster from where it worked over the Clapham to Low Gill (via Ingleton) line, then over Shap to Penrith. From here the train ventured on to ex-NER territory to Kirkby Stephen. The itinerary then took in Tebay, Hincaster Junction, Sandside to Arnside and the Lakeside Branch from Ulverston. The final leg through Carnforth and Hest Bank was to Morecambe Promenade before returning to Lancaster Castle and retracing the outward route arriving back at 9.02pm. The 300 mile round trip cost 35/- and a cafeteria car was provided.

29th MAY 1960 ● **J. DAVENPORT**

Ex-LNER Pacific No 60007 Sir Nigel Gresley was a prestigious visitor. She is passing through off the Cheetham Hill Loop prior to working a railtour from Manchester Exchange to London Paddington and back. The loco arrived at Newton Heath shed for servicing the previous day light engine from Aberdeen Ferryhill.

22nd OCTOBER 1965 ● **R.S. GREENWOOD**

The RCTS Four Counties Rail Tour produced a Gorton J11/3 No **64420** one fine Autumn Saturday morning. The loco had received special attention with burnished brass beading on the splashers, the workplates picked out in green and fresh numerals applied to the cab sides. The tour covered certain lines in Lancashire, Cheshire, Derbyshire and Staffordshire which had recently lost or never had passenger services. The ex-GC veteran was responsible for the first leg of the itinerary. Travelling out via Miles Platting and Ashton Moss Junction to Guide Bridge, the train traversed the Waterside Branch before proceeding via Godley Junction and on to CLC metals. Upon reaching Northenden Junction, Driver Davies and Fireman Wolstencroft handed over to Stockport Edgeley's Fowler 2-6-4T No 42372 with Driver Lee and Fireman Carroll now in charge.

23rd SEPTEMBER 1961 ● **G. HARROP**

An outing organised by the Stephenson Locomotive Society involved Jubilee 4-6-0 No **45698** *Mars*. By 1965 the numbers of this popular class left in service were dwindling fast and it was perhaps appropriate that *Mars* was entrusted to the working. A long time resident of Bank Hall depot, she regularly passed through Victoria Station with the 10.30am Liverpool Exchange - Newcastle dining car express during the 1950's, working as far as York. After servicing at Clifton depot, *Mars* would return to Merseyside with the 5.10pm ex-Newcastle - Liverpool after relieving a Gateshead loco, often a Pacific. This particular duty was usually shared with stablemates No 45717 *Dauntless,* No 45719 *Glorious* and unrebuilt Patriot - un-named No 45517. The loco had arrived at Newton Heath depot light engine the previous day in readiness for a sentimental journey up the Calder Valley as far as Wakefield (Kirkgate), although the train was eventually destined for Whitby, This head-on view shows No 45698 bringing the empty stock from Ordsall Lane Carriage Sidings and into Platform 14. A group of enthusiasts are on the adjoining platform, some recording its arrival by film, others on audio tape. A locomotive already secured in preservation at the time, ex-LNER K4 2-6-0 No 3442 *The Great Marquess,* took the train forward from Wakefield. **6th MARCH 1965** ● **G. HARROP**

Driver Ken Royle and Fireman Bobby Burns were the Newton Heath men selected for the turn. The redoubtable Royle recalls requests for a fiery departure out of Victoria by enthusiasts but otherwise logged a trouble free trip. After stabling the loco on Wakefield Shed they came home 'on the cushions'. **6th MARCH 1965** ● **KEN ROYLE COLLECTION**

THREE COUNTIES SPECIAL

This tour was the first of a series by the fledgling *'Manchester Rail Travel Society'* whose efforts would eventually lead to preservation and restoration to full working order of Jinty 3F 0-6-0T No 47383. Trafford Park provided Stanier Class 4 2-6-4T No **42644** for the first stage of the railtour *(see itinerary)*. On the previous Friday evening a bunch of members set about cleaning the loco at Newton Heath shed under the watchful eye of the Foreman Cleaner. They then retired to the nearby 'Dean Brook Inn' to raise a glass or five in anticipation of the success of the following days outing.

**12th NOVEMBER 1966 ● PETER HOOD/
BERNARD CRICK COLLECTION**

MANCHESTER RAIL • • •
• • • TRAVEL SOCIETY

Treasurer,
4, Kirkstone Road,
Moston,
Manchester, 10.

Secretary,
7, Claife Avenue,
Moston,
Manchester, 10.

"THREE COUNTIES SPECIAL"

Dear Sir,

Thank you for your enquiry requesting details of the "Three Counties Special" and I hope the following information will interest you. The tour covers over 125 miles of track in three counties and employs five locomotives.

The tour departs Manchester Victoria, platform 11 middle at 10-00am behind 'Stanier' tank, 42656, or another member of the class, via Dean Lane, Oldham and on to Rochdale. Taking the Bolton line from Rochdale, the train of four coaches proceeds to Bury Knowsley Street and Bolton Street. The train then continues to Bacup, which was the first line to be wholly converted to 'dmu' workings in the country.

At Bacup the Stanier tank runs arround the four coaches and hauls the train back to Bury Bolton Street. Here the tank is replaced by two 0-6-0T "Jinties", 47202 and 47383, the former being the last 3F condensing tank locomotive, the loco-motive we hope to preserve from your support of our societies tours. The pair travel double headed to Stockport Edgeley via Clifton Junction, Manchester Victoria and Exchange, Miles Platting and Droylsden.. At Stockport the pair of 3F's are exchanged for an Ivatt tank 41220 (Push and Pull fitted) and continues to Buxton, via Disley. At Buxton we change to one of the last two J94's 68012 which after a run arround at Miller's Dale takes us back along the Midland Railway Co. line into Manchester Central at 16-45. Manchester Victoria 10-00; Bacup 11-42/12-10; Bury Bolton Street 12-40/12-55; Stockport Edgeley 13-45/14-05; Buxton 14-54/15-10; Millers Dale 15-35/15-52; Manchester Central 16-45.

Last of all the fare, 40/-d, to be pulled by some of the vastly disappearing locomotives of our time. HELP TO SAVE 47202 NOW.

Please reserve me _____ place(s) on the "Three Counties Special" on Saturday November 12th, 1966, to Bacup, Bury Stockport and Buxton from Manchester hauled by Motive Power as above.

I enclose remittance to the value of _____ for the train fare(s)

I also enclose (1) one S.A.E. for tickets. (2) two S.A.E. for ticket and receipt for remittance.

Name (Block Letters) _____

Address _____

RETURN THIS SECTION TO B. H. CRICK, ESQ., 4, KIRKSTONE ROAD, MOSTON, MANCHESTER, 10.

EARLY DIESELS

A common sight in and around the bays was **M55988**, a motor parcels van built by Gloucester R.C. & W. Co in 1958. These powerful units were fitted with three sets of double doors on either side. She is about to depart from Platform 17 with a string of vans in tow bound for Oldham Clegg Street. M55988 spent most weekdays tootling around the locality before being withdrawn from service in 1976.

22nd JUNE 1960 ● GRAHAM WHITEHEAD

By the summer of 1962, all semaphores around Victoria Station had been replaced with colour light signals. Well in advance of their removal, diesel locomotives had become a common sight here. Initially they worked in from Blackpool on filling-in turns off the London Euston-Blackpool trains, one of the first jobs regularly entrusted to the English Electric Type 4's. Len Brooks, the guard, had walked the length of the train to converse with the driver of **D231** before getting the 'right away' from Platform 15 with empty stock to Red Bank Carriage Sidings. In the early diesel days it was common practice for locos to carry a shedplate beneath the number. This example was based at 8A Edge Hill (Liverpool). Meanwhile Stanier Class Five 4-6-0 No **44890** drifts in under Cheetham Hill Road Bridge with stock for a Westbound train.

22nd JUNE 1960 ● GRAHAM WHITEHEAD

Rebuilding of the ex-LNWR side of London Road Station started on 25th April 1960, when the ex-GC side had been completed. LNW section main line trains were diverted to Victoria (or Exchange in the case of the 'Mancunian') via Reddish South and Droylsden Junction or to Central Station via Middlewich and Northwich. English Electric Type 4 Diesel No **D219** has left Exchange earlier than the 9.45am time from London Road in order to maintain the existing schedule south of Crewe. The train did not stop there, however, and remained diesel hauled when normal service was resumed on 12th September 1960 at the re-named Piccadilly Station, at which time the Manchester - Crewe section was electrified.

4TH JUNE 1960 ● T. LEWIS

The Hellifield services brought further variety into the station. The Midland Railway locomotive departing from Platform 12 is Modified 2P 4-4-0 No **384** - in immaculate condition with her red livery enhanced by burnished buffers, smokebox hinges and surround. She was originally built by Johnson in 1890 but the class were considered to be under-boilered. They were extensively rebuilt by Deeley from 1904 onwards, receiving larger cabs, plain splashers (replacing the decorative variety) and, of course, bigger boilers. This particular loco has also acquired a Belpaire firebox and extended smokebox, further modifications that were not extended to all the class.

c.1910 ● **N. PREEDY COLLECTION**

LMS Hughes/Fowler 'Crab' 2-6-0 No 13014 awaits departure. The glazed canopy extending from the overall roof at the east end of Platforms 14 and 15 suffered from the ravages of war - and was subsequently demolished. Note the Crossley advert - a reminder of the established Manchester manufacturing company long associated with the Corporation Transport Department.

JULY 1931 ● **E.R. MORTEN**

The Midland influence continued throughout the LMS and into the early BR period and visits by the 'Compounds' were commonplace. A low sun nicely highlights the rivet detail of No **1087** whilst the driver looks back down his train, perhaps in search of a green flag. The loco was a stranger, residing at Leeds (Holbeck) Depot.

18th OCTOBER 1947 ● **H.C. CASSERLEY**

One of the Wigan (L&Y) Stanier 2-6-4 tanks, No 42645 awaits departure with a stopping train to Southport. Although the combination of 11, 11 Middle & Manchester Exchange's No 3 produced the longest platform in the country, relatively few passenger trains used the Victoria end in the latter years of steam. The final departure of the day was as early as 7pm, again bound for Southport and from that time onwards it became a hive of activity with all manner of parcels and newspaper trains coming and going until well into the early hours.

8th AUGUST 1963 ● GRAHAM WHITEHEAD

The Divisional Engineer's Special trains on the Central Division were entrusted in the latter years of steam to a couple of Ivatt Moguls. Nos 46411 and **46437** were kept in excellent condition by the maintenance staff at Newton Heath for such duties. Driver 'Slow Line' Jones, standing on Platform 11 middle and Fireman Frank Wood are awaiting the arrival of dignitaries from the nearby Hunts Bank offices.

23rd AUGUST 1966 ● TOM HEAVYSIDE

An unidentified Standard Caprotti Class Five awaits departure with an excursion. In common with Platform 11, this middle section also saw little passenger activity. The glass screen offered a degree of protection from the elements and served to keep the newspapers dry!

21st JULY 1967 ● PAUL JORDAN

In January 1960, Britannia Pacific Nos 70045 *Lord Rowallan* and 70048 *The Territorial Army 1908 - 1958* arrived from Camden and thus became the first Class 7 locos to be allocated to Newton Heath. Nos 70014 *Iron Duke,* 70015 *Apollo* and 70049 *Solway Firth* arrived during the same year as it was considered that the shed needed larger engines to cope with the new timetable. The Jubilees had continued to find difficulty in maintaining time on the accelerated Up and Down evening trains between Glasgow and Manchester and double heading had become commonplace. The introduction of these Pacifics hardly improved matters and all five were transferred away to Neasden in September 1961. No **70045 *Lord Rowallan*** blows off impatiently in Platform 12 having been relegated to secondary duties. She is about to depart with the 5.15pm to Blackpool Central, calling at Bolton then all stations except Salwick.   **8th JANUARY 1961** ● **GRAHAM WHITEHEAD**

Escaping steam between engine and tender is a cause for concern for the driver of Crewe North Britannia Pacific No **70052 *Firth of Tay*.** A split in the steam heating hose was the problem and will be marked on the report card for attention. The train has reached its destination and the empty stock will shortly be taken out of Platform 15 'round the curve' to Red Bank Carriage Sidings. The 'Heath Robinson' contraption to the right of the loco on the adjacent platform is a handcart based wooden extending platform. Dating from L&Y days, it was originally used to replace high level gas mantles and lamps in later years. It was a familiar, yet taken for granted, sight around the station for many years.

8th APRIL 1965 ● **BERNARD CRICK**

WALLSIDE PILOTS

LMS Fairburn 2-6-4T No 2208 stands on duty. Although a 26A loco at the time, by BR days she would be away, north of the border to Motherwell working on local passenger trains rather than pilot work. The lack of attention to the structure of the building throughout the 1950's is evident here. Note the missing glass panels within the wall.

15th AUGUST 1946 ● **P.J. HUGHES**

Stanier Class 4 2-6-4T No 42640

29th SEPTEMBER 1962 ● **P. HUTCHINSON**

Standard 2-6-4T No 80049 and ex-L&Y 0-6-0 No 52159

1st SEPTEMBER 1956 ●
PAUL SHACKCLOTH COLLECTION

Ex-Midland 4F 0-6-0 No 43979 and ex-LMS 4F 0-6-0 No 44431

15th JULY 1964 ● **J. PEDEN COLLECTION**

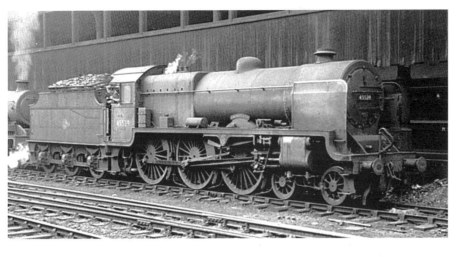

Patriot 4-6-0 No 45539 *E.C. Trench*

DECEMBER 1962 ● D. HAMPSON

Ivatt 2-6-0 No 46437

DECEMBER 1964 ● PAUL SHACKCLOTH

Portraits of the Wallside Pilot locos were common, recorded by many cameramen from the convenience of No 11 Platform. The early morning offered the light to its best advantage here. Fairburn 2-6-4 tank No **42696** is awaiting the passage of Standard 9F 2-10-0 No **92162** with a lengthy mixed goods train before providing assistance up the bank. Between these two locos stands Ivatt Class 2 2-6-0 No **46449** which will move forward and await the next train.

14th JUNE 1964 ● H.C. CASSERLEY

The L&YR, owners of Victoria Station, always boasted that the standard of their in-house catering facility was unsurpassed by any of its rivals. The restaurant, or to give it its proper title, 'Grill Room' was a rather grand affair, situated at the end of the concourse and backing on to the original 1844 building, almost facing the ticket barrier offering access to Platforms 11 - 17. The main entrance looked directly down Hunts Bank approach. By 1910 the 'Grill Room' was generally considered to be one of the finest eating houses in the city. The L&YR were justifiably proud of this reputation and for similar accolades at the Liverpool Exchange Hotel. The room, seen here set for luncheon with hardly a napkin out of place, was decorated with Terrazzo tiling and had a distinctive domed roof. Many of the catering staff lived on the premises.

c.1910 ● JOHN RYAN COLLECTION

GRILL ROOM AND BUFFET

A smaller buffet facility could be found on Platform 12. Both premises were licensed for the sale of intoxicating liquors to be consumed on the premises only. Many passengers would have enjoyed a pint of draught bass served in those distinctive fluted handled pots whilst waiting for their train. Sandwiches and pies were usually available here whilst bowls of soup were popular, particularly with the trainspotting brigade and represented good value. Luncheon vouchers were readily accepted and prominent on the counter, through the window, is a milk machine. The 'Drinka-Pinta-Milka-Day' advertising campaign was in full swing as was British Rail's new Inter-City image, the billboard poster reading 'New Trans-Pennine services give you speed, comfort and economy'. The time is 2.15pm and the lights are already on giving a fair indication of the gloomy atmosphere passengers had to endure. The close proximity of the 'Wallside Pilots' hardly helped matters.

9th DECEMBER 1967 ● PAUL SHACKCLOTH

Considered by many to be the principal train of the day. The 10.30am ex-Liverpool Exchange - Newcastle service possibly gained this reputation by being the only restaurant car train to regularly work over the ex-L&Y system in BR days. The scheduled departure from Platform 13 was at 11.28am and a banking loco was usually provided. However, certain Bank Hall men, proud of their Jubilees, often declined this assistance and got smartly away without the customary 'crow' on the whistle. The end result was a Lanky 'A' 0-6-0 class in hot pursuit. These activities were carefully observed by East Junction signalmen who would then inform their Footbridge counterparts to wave the red flag ordering the loco to give up the chase.   **27th JULY 1957 ● ERIC BENTLEY**

On Summer Saturdays in the 1950's and early 1960's, trainspotters were actively discouraged from loitering on the platforms. Purchase of a 2d Platform Ticket often met with a stubborn refusal at the barriers of both Victoria and Exchange. If one was lucky enough to arrive at a through platform, it was possible to get through the day undetected. Alternatively, the inspector could hardly deny access if one presented a local cheap day single ticket. The platform enders tended to congregate on numbers 12 and 13 in the depths of winter as the warm, inviting buffet was situated there. Conditions underfoot were treacherous this day, but three intrepid souls have braved the elements and were rewarded with the passage of Stanier Class Five No **44845** making for Red Bank with a parcels train.   **9th DECEMBER 1967 ● PAUL SHACKCLOTH**

When Belle Vue (26G) shed closed on 14th April 1956, Newton Heath took over all the workings, apart from the Gowhole Pilots which became Heaton Mersey's responsibility. Sixteen locos were re-allocated including these two, Stanier Class Fives, Nos **44803** and **44845**. Both locos were to remain in service until the official closure of the depot to steam on Monday, July 1st 1968. No 44803 is on 'Wallside Pilot' duty whilst No 44845 awaits the signal with a parcels train.

9th DECEMBER 1967 ● PAUL SHACKCLOTH

The view from the luggage bridge where two Class Fives are caught acting out the last rites. No **44809** draws mail vans away from Platform 6 whilst No **45268** is the solitary Wallside Pilot on the penultimate day of regular steam operation here. Over the years more than a few locomen have nipped over into the refreshment room for a 'quick half' between banking turns. It was conveniently situated directly opposite the stabling point on Platform 12.

29th JUNE 1968 ● DAVE JESSOP

Between 1889 and 1918, Horwich Works built 385 examples of the Class 27 0-6-0 locomotive. Those that survived until the early 1960's were true veterans and their longevity in service reflected a successful design - a testament to the man responsible, the Chief Mechanical Engineer of the L&YR at the time, Mr. J. A. Aspinall. Some 28 members served in the Great War and No **52239** was one such loco. After entering service in July 1894 as L&Y No 469, she was requisitioned and renumbered by the Railway Operating Department as 6711, seeing service on the 'Western Front' between March 1917 and June 1919. The hole in the buffer beam was for fixing the side chains - a minor modification deemed necessary by the French railway authorities. She adopted LMS No 12239 at the Grouping before her BR number and was withdrawn in February 1956, after 62 years faithful service.

JULY 1951   ●   W.R.P. LEES

Although Ex-LNWR engines were a common sight passing through Victoria Station, they rarely entered the platforms. An unidentified 0-6-2 Webb Coal Tank arrives with a portion of a train from Stockport Edgeley. The veteran loco has travelled by way of Denton and Droylsden Junctions and Miles Platting. After depositing her passengers on Platform 11, she would then proceed to Ordsall Lane Carriage Sidings with the empty stock before moving on to Patricroft depot for servicing.

JULY 1931   ●   E. R. MORTEN

The depths of a winter gripped in snow often created dramatic photographic images - but it also created extra work for the station staff. Whilst the running of trains to time may not have been their direct responsibility, it was a porter's job to prevent the water columns from freezing over. At least three such columns were in-situ at the east end of Platforms 14/15 and 16/17 as well as the west end of Number 12. All had strategically placed braziers offering relief during periods such as this. They had burned for many years but this was to be their last - they, too, would soon be redundant. The heat haze conspires to distort the front numberplate of Stanier Class 5 4-6-0 No **45342**.

9th DECEMBER 1967 ●
PAUL SHACKCLOTH

Nearly three years after the celebrated pair of named Class 5's came south, a trio of more low profile engines arrived from north of the border. Fairburn Class 4 2-6-4 tanks Nos 42696/7/8 came from Motherwell, Ardrossan and Greenock respectively in exchange for three Standard versions, Nos 80044/60/61 which had moved to Scottish sheds, no doubt to simplify the situation regarding spares. No **42696** is caught standing just out of the shadow of Cheetham Hill Road Bridge - she has been recently overhauled at Derby and is in ex-works condition.

8th SEPTEMBER 1960 ● **PETER FITTON**

EAST END STATION PILOTS

In contrast, the condition of Ivatt Class 2 2-6-0 No 46449 somehow matches that of its surroundings. The loco was seemingly in far better mechanical than external order for it soldiered on in service for a further 21 months and is pictured here in action, marshalling a single coach through Platform No 16.

9th AUGUST 1965 ● **GORDON COLTAS**

The class leader of the BR 'Clan' Pacifics, No 72000 *Clan Buchanan* awaits departure from Platform 11 Middle with the morning 'Glasgow' via Bolton. These 6P/5F engines were considered somewhat of a failure both in terms of performance and capital expenditure and only 10 were constructed despite plans for more. They were confined to the Scottish Region where Nos 72000-4 worked almost exclusively out of Polmadie (Glasgow) depot All five were withdrawn en-masse in December 1962 after exactly 11 years in service. After a period of storage, first at Polmadie and then at Parkhead they were eventually cut up at Darlington between February and March 1964. The remaining locos (Nos 72005-9) enjoyed a slightly longer innings working out of Carlisle (Kingmoor) depot. **10th SEPTEMBER 1959 ● R.S. GREENWOOD**

The 1.30pm train to Glasgow finds itself in the hands of Polmadie's ex-LMS Royal Scot Class 4-6-0 No **46105 *Cameron Highlander*.** The rear portion went forward to Edinburgh Princes Street after splitting at Carstairs. A third train left from Platform 11 Middle at 4.30pm for Glasgow Central but this appeared in the Manchester Exchange timetable as it travelled over ex-LNWR metals via Wigan North Western. An unidentified Class Five is reversing on to coaching stock in the adjacent number 15 Platform. **21st FEBRUARY 1962 ● R.S. GREENWOOD**

On this occasion the morning ex-Glasgow Central to Manchester Victoria train was in the hands of a Polmadie engine and men - the Glasgow turns usually involved working alternate days with their Newton Heath counterparts. In early BR days the ex-Caledonian depot preferred to use one of its five Royal Scot 4-6-0's (Nos 46102/4/5/7/21), but from December 1951 until full dieselisation of the service in 1963, their BR 'Clan' (Nos 72000-4) and later the 'Britannia' Pacifics (Nos 70050-54) put in regular appearances. No **46102 *Black Watch*** gets the empty stock away towards Cheetham Hill Carriage Sidings before proceeding light engine to Newton Heath shed. This was a lodging turn with both men and loco working home with the following morning's 9.30am Glasgow service.   **APRIL 1962** ● **R.S. GREENWOOD COLLECTION**

The SSO 3.25pm Blackpool Central - Cleethorpes was routed via Manchester Victoria without a scheduled stop. An interesting choice of motive power is ex-LMS 4F 0-6-0 No **44311**, a loco adapted for snowplough duties. It was unusual to find such extras passing through the platforms, which was an indication of the high volume of through traffic that day. The loco will work the train up Miles Platting bank via Philips Park as far as Midland Junction where it will hand over to electric traction for the onward journey to Sheffield Victoria via Woodhead. The train will then revert to steam haulage for the final leg to Cleethorpes, probably behind a Darnall loco - perhaps a B1 or K3, or if the shed were as equally hard pushed as Newton Heath that day, maybe a J11 would be pressed into service!   **2nd APRIL 1960** ● **PETER FITTON**

PARCELS TRAFFIC

This view looking along a deserted Platform 12 is a far cry from the scene often witnessed here. It regularly thronged with passengers and was arguably Victoria's most used through platform over the years, dealing with a high percentage of the departures for the Fylde coast. Ivatt Class 2MT No **46501** resumes its position on the 'Wallside' after a spell of banking duty. By 1965 Newton Heath had a number of 'Mickey Mouses' on the books which were regularly used for this work. Immediately behind the loco is a two-car Cravens DMU set on the short spur in front of West Junction box. The lines to the immediate right are those avoiding Exchange Station. In the background stands the smaller Irwell Bridge box alongside which was a turntable and parachute water tank offering a quick service facility for the suburban traffic to and from the west. Parcels vans occupy Platform 11 middle whilst Exchange station looms in the background. The truncated silhouetted roof offers a stark reminder that it once spanned the through roads before the war.   **2nd APRIL 1966 ● ERIC BENTLEY**

A stroll down to the westerly end of Platforms 14 and 15 offered cameraman Tom Heavyside this interesting view. Stanier Class Five 4-6-0 No **44949** is at the head of an eastbound parcels train routed through Platform 13. The stock comprises a typical motley collection of newspaper vans, no two seemingly being the same. Prominent also in the view is West Junction signal box which has suffered a broken window pane. Note the bay window middle section designed to offer the train recorder greater visibility. The screen wall protecting Platform 11 Middle from the elements has also suffered similar damage. In the background are the distinctive curves of Exchange Station roof.

24th JUNE 1967 ● TOM HEAVYSIDE

One of the busiest platforms within the Victoria complex was No 16 which, being adjacent to the Parcels Depot, naturally dealt with large volumes of this traffic. Incoming long distance passenger trains from the West (including the Glasgow services) were also received but very few passenger trains departed from here. The exception came during the rebuilding period in 1960 of Manchester London Road and the influx of diversionary traffic. The 8.08am and the 5.28pm *Comet* were restaurant car express trains for London Euston and in addition, two more left within 12 minutes of each other on weekdays. The 5.35pm all stations to Todmorden was followed by the 5.47pm Birmingham New Street. Stanier Class Five No **45226** runs in with empty newspaper vans, passing through the most westerly part of the platforms which appear to be used as a dump for, amongst other things, unserviceable parcels trolleys.

2nd APRIL 1967 ● JEFF CLOUGH

PLATFORM 16

Traffic arrived and departed from each direction and these parcels trains often realised an interesting variety of motive power. One of the unsightly Caprotti variants from within the large Stanier Class Five family was No **44746** from Longsight shed. Examples from the 'Wessie' shed on the south side of the city were considered extremely rare birds.

c.1959 ● PAUL SHACKCLOTH COLLECTION

Ivatt Mogul No 46437 drifts in with more vans. A mound of parcels on a pair of trolleys standing on the adjacent No 15 platform appear to be rather near the edge! To the right of the loco is the ramshackle covered approach which sloped down to a 24ft wide subway connecting Platforms 11 and 17. No doubt many older passengers will recall the thunderous roar and vibration when a train passed overhead, especially one of the Hull or Newcastle services getting away from Exchange Station and going 'flat out' for Miles Platting bank.

24th OCTOBER 1964 ● G. HARROP

VICTORIA BY NIGHT

Class 'C' engine head lamps burning brightly are carried by Stanier Class Five No **45076**. Apparently this loco was a temperamental performer in her later days and was often shy of steam. With safety valves blowing, this was hardly the case on this occasion! The Newton Heath engine is standing in Platform 17 awaiting departure for Oldham Clegg Street Parcels Depot with an evening train.

FEBRUARY 1968 ● TED PARKER

A distinctly grubby Fairburn 2-6-4T No 42054 further blackens the soot-ridden brick wall alongside Platform 17 whilst employed on pilot duty. The loco's stay was short lived. It came and went within a four-month period, being withdrawn from Newton Heath in July 1964.

2nd APRIL 1964 ● GRAHAM WHITEHEAD

11	00 SO	8	All stations to Oldham and Rochdale.
	00 SO	13	Moston, and all stations, except Luddendenfoot, to Halifax Town.
	05 SX	13FSX 17FO	}Moston, and all stations to Todmorden.
	05 FO	12	To 12th August inclusive—Fleetwood (for Isle of Man).
	10 FO	15	To 19th August inclusive—Norwich Thorpe, Yarmouth Vauxhall.
	10 SO	14	All stations via Atherton Central to Wigan.
	12 SX	12	Bolton, Darwen, Blackburn, Accrington, Rose Grove, and all stations to Colne.
	14	10	London Euston. CONVEYS 1st and 2nd CLASS SLEEPING CAR PASSENGERS ONLY.
	15	14	All stations to Bolton.
	23 FO	13	To 19th August inclusive—Hereford, Pontypool Road, Taunton, Exeter, Dawlish, Teignmouth, Newton Abbot, Kingskerswell, Torre, Torquay, Paignton.
	30	7	All stations to Oldham and Rochdale.
	36	14	Stockport Edgeley, Macclesfield Hibel Road, Stoke-on-Trent, Derby Midland, Leicester London Road, Market Harborough, Kettering, Wellingborough Midland Road, Bedford Midland Road, Luton Midland Road, London St. Pancras.

The fascinating period when Victoria dealt with the diversionary traffic from London Road has already been mentioned, but a small section of the summer timetable of 1960 reveals added assortment. I doubt whether many enthusiasts ventured down to the station between the hours of 11pm and midnight on Friday evenings, but those that did would have been rewarded by a hive of activity. Extra departures to Fleetwood, Yarmouth Vauxhall and Paignton left within minutes of each other and of further interest is the sleeping car service to London Euston only, departing at 11.14pm, which was stabled in Platform 10!

An impressive close up of Hughes 'Crab' 2-6-0 No **2711.** With a power classification of five for mixed traffic, these locos were primarily intended for fast goods. Their 5' 6" diameter driving wheels excluded them from working the smartly timed trains but they were versatile engines and came into their own on the more sedate excursion work. The 245 members of the class were spread far and wide over the LMS system - from Ayr and Ardrossan in Scotland to Crewe South to Cricklewood (London). Although introduced in 1926 they were, essentially, an L&Y design and a number of the early examples ran out of Newton Heath depot. The transfer of No 2711 from 26A to Aintree in March 1957 would have resulted in the loco being used almost exclusively on freight work for the remainder of her days.

20th JULY 1947 ● **K. FAIREY**

VICTORIA STATION - WEST END

The 10.10am from York has arrived on New Year's Day behind a Doncaster B1 4-6-0 No **61155.** This wasn't uncommon as York often 'borrowed' this class of loco for working the train and Darlington examples were also observed. After stabling the empty stock at Irlam Carriage Sidings, the ex-LNER engine spent the afternoon on Agecroft shed. She then returned home with the 5.10pm train. An unidentified Stanier 2-6-4T stands in the adjoining Platform.

1st JANUARY 1959 ●
R.S. GREENWOOD

The principal westbound routes served Liverpool, Wigan, Southport, Preston, Blackpool and Fleetwood. Those to the north went to Lancaster, Barrow, Workington, Carlisle and Glasgow. Trains to Hellifield ran by way of Bolton and Blackburn whilst the intensive suburban services were to Bury, Bacup, Accrington and Colne and to Rochdale via the Oldham loop. Rochdale could also be reached via Castleton before travelling onwards to Todmorden, Halifax, Bradford and Leeds or to Wakefield, Normanton, Goole and York by way of the Calder Valley main line. Other local services were to Stalybridge and Stockport (Edgeley) for connections to London Euston and all points south. Rebuilt Patriot 4-6-0 No **45522** ***Prestatyn*** stands at Platform 14 with the 1.30pm to Carlisle. Not only was this the last of the Patriot class to be rebuilt in 1949, it was the only one of its kind to have graced 26A's books.

3rd APRIL 1963 ● **GRAHAM WHITEHEAD**

LMS 0-6-0 No 4460 awaits departure with the 12.45pm all stations (except Salford) to Blackburn whilst Stanier 2-6-4 tank No **2656** moves its train away with the 12.37pm to Liverpool Exchange.　　**11th FEBRUARY 1948** ● **H.C. CASSERLEY**

Agecroft 'Crab' 2-6-0 No 42868 is about to move its empty stock to Irlam Carriage Sidings after having brought a stopping train in from Normanton via the Calder Valley line.

c.1956 ● **A. HAYNES**

Three trains left Victoria simultaneously at 5.40pm on weekdays. An all stations to Greenfield departed from the bays and standing in Platform 12 is Standard Class 4MT 4-6-0 No **75015** with a Southport residential, calling at Wigan Wallgate only. Stanier 2-6-4 tank No **42545** will leave Platform 14 before calling at Bolton, Darwen, Blackburn then all stations to Hellifield. Stanier Class Five No **45225** stands on the short spur immediately in front of Victoria West Junction signalbox.　　**11th SEPTEMBER 1958** ● **C.A. APPLETON**

By 1959, Leicester Central Shed had been transferred from the ER to the LMR and recoded 15E. A merry-go-round of loco transfers then ensued. In September of that year the depot received five Standard Class 5's from Holbeck leaving its ex-LNER B1 4-6-0's surplus to requirements. Nos 61008/ 61201/61269/61298 and 61369 were moved to the ex-L&Y depot at Agecroft between August and October. They, in turn, ousted that depot's Crab 2-6-0's on the Manchester - Normanton and York stopping trains. They were decidedly unpopular with the Agecroft men and were transferred away early in 1962 by which time Jubilees, no longer required on the Midland main line, arrived from the Sheffield area. Here, No **61369** drifts through the middle road still awaiting its 26B shedplate although the code has been painted within the recess of the backing plate.

17th OCTOBER 1959 ● R. S. GREENWOOD

DIVERTED TRAFFIC

An Ordsall Lane to Mottram freight passes though the station hauled by ex-LNER J39/1 No **64718.** This was a typical diverted working due to the electrification work at Manchester London Road and its environs. The train would normally have taken the flatter route by way of Castlefield Junction and Oxford Road Station before passing through London Road's M.S.J.&A platforms. This lightweight train, however, should pose few problems for the Gorton engine on the ascent to Miles Platting Junction.

18th APRIL 1959 ● P. HUTCHINSON

Another diverted freight brings a member of the ex-GC 04 2-8-0 class through Victoria showing through freight, Class 'H' head-lamps. The damp and dismal conditions seemed to be in keeping with the state of many of Gorton's large allocation of freight locomotives. This particular example, No **63598** was a long standing resident and was one of the last nine there, all of which were withdrawn in November 1962. She is working across the city with a mixture of wagons from Dewsnap to Ordsall Lane.

28th DECEMBER 1959 ● R. S. GREENWOOD

The Saturday 11.15am stopping train for Blackpool North and Fleetwood stands in Platform 12 shortly before departure. Class Five 4-6-0 No **45436,** impatiently blowing off steam, creates the the kind of stirring sight so often observed in and around the station. With no traffic momentarily passing on the through lines, the morning sun shows off this example of Stanier's most productive class to great effect. She was a Blackpool engine for many years and, as such, a common visitor to the city.   **5th MARCH 1960 ● ERIC BENTLEY**

Another common visitor was Bank Hall's unique Class Five No **44767**. She was the only member of the class built with piston valves actuated by two sets of outside Stephenson Link Motion. The valve gear is clearly evident in this low angle view of the loco getting its Liverpool train away from Platform 11. Other detail differences included Timken roller bearings to all axles, manganese steel liners to its axle box guides, double blast pipe and chimney, rocking grate, self-cleaning smokebox and electric lighting. Although modified in later years, the loco is happily preserved in working order and now carries the name 'George Stephenson'.   **c.1950 ● ARTHUR BENDELL**

IMAGES AT
VICTORIA STATION

1967 ● PAUL SHACKCLOTH

MILLER STREET

The unique Pilcher Car No 125 operating on Service No 51 from Oxford Road to Miller Street. Of this final batch of 38 cars built by the Corporation at their Hyde Road Works between 1930 and 1932, 37 had plain axle bearings in rectangular axleboxes. No 125, however, had roller-bearing axleboxes supposedly designed to last for ever! She was selected for an enthusiasts' tour of the Manchester area in 1939 for which purpose she received a thorough repaint. The demise of the tramway system saw the eventual transfer away of all the Pilcher Cars. No 125 found a new home in Edinburgh, being one of eleven sold to the Corporation between October 1946 and June 1948. Note the sign directing passengers towards Victoria Station on the ventilation column above the gentlemen's public conveniences.

25th AUGUST 1938 ● W. A. CAMWELL

A Salford Corporation Daimler CVG6 crosses Cheetham Hill Road bridge on the joint No 35 service from Bury. The structure was 22 yards wide and catered for the extension of the tramway system towards Cheetham Hill. It was completed in 1904 which coincided with other major developments in and around Victoria Station. Strangeways tower looms over the *Paramount Garage* at the corner of Great Bridge Street. Behind the deep parapet on the west side of the bridge is the Railway Signal & Telegraph Depot, opening in 1911 and built on ground once occupied by the Manchester Union Workhouse. A BR poster is offering trips to Blackpool for seven shillings return whilst, as if anybody needed reminding, the graffiti of the day told its own story.

1959 ● MANCHESTER CENTRAL LIBRARY

BUS SERVICES CROSSING CHEETHAM HILL ROAD BRIDGE IN 1959:

No	Route	Garage
4	Cannon Street - Heywood - Bamford	QR
26	Moston - Blackley - Crumpsall - Cheetham Hill - Waterloo Road - Cannon Street*	QR
35	Cannon Street - Cheetham Hill - Whitefield - Bury	QR, FR & B
49	Crumpsall Green - Cheetham Hill Road - Cannon Street*	QR
59	Cannon Street - Cheetham Hill - Middleton - Oldham - Shaw	QR & O
60	Cannon Street - Blackley Estate *(circular via Cheetham Hill Road & Rochdale Road)*	QR
62	Chorlton - Albert Square - Cheetham Hill Road - Heaton Park	QR
75	Greenheys - Albert Square - Cheetham Hill Road - Heaton Park	QR & PR
78	Fallowfield - Albert Square - Hightown	QR & PR
81	Southern Cemetery - Chorlton - Albert Square - Hightown	QR & PR

Garages: QR - Queens Road   PR - Princess Road   FR - Frederick Road
O - Oldham (Wallshaw Street)   B - Bury (Rochdale Road)   * *Inward journeys only*

The service between Greenheys, Platt Lane and Corporation Street succumbed from trolley to motorbus operation on 1st June 1959 because the land occupied by the terminal loop at the end of Miller Street was needed for the development of the new CIS building. The replacement No 123 service covered the same 4 mile route and still operated out of Hyde Road Garage who tended to use Leyland PD2/12s (Nos 3330-69). The No 213 was short lived, taking over from route No 30 on 21st April 1952 which in turn had replaced the 51 tram twelve years earlier. *(Left)* Briitish United Traction No **1360** (ONE 760), nearing its destination, is pictured entering Miller Street from Swan Street. She was the shortest lived of all the Corporation trolleybuses, lasting a mere 8 years and 2 months in service (February 1956 - April 1964) before being sold to Autospares of Bingley for scrap. *(Right)* Another BUT No **1317** (ONE 717) is about to turn off Rochdale Road and follow a Crossley bus, in earlier livery, into Thompson Street on the outward journey on the penultimate day of service. The shell of the new general produce depot within the Oldham Road complex brings up the rear. **3rd APRIL 1959 ● 29th MAY 1959 ● P.J. THOMPSON**

If you regularly occupied the front seat of a bus which travelled along Rochdale Road, then this photograph will rekindle fond memories. Owned by the NWGB, Andrew Barclay 0-4-0 No **2197 *William H Oldfield MP*** is crossing the main road on the level from the Oldham Road Goods Yard at Sudell Street into the Rochdale Road Gas Works complex. The yard man, whose responsibility was to open and then secure the gates on either side of the road, had brought traffic in each direction to a halt by enthusiastically waving a red flag, an operation he carried out several times a day. The volume of road transport at the time created little inconvenience. Rochdale Road Garage lies just behind the trolleybus awaiting a clear road for the run into town down Shude Hill to Church Street.

13th SEPTEMBER 1952 ● C.A. APPLETON

Driver training from Queens Road Garage brings Leyland PD1/3 No **3101** (JNA 402) out of town along Great Ducie Street whilst an unidentified Leyland Titan PD2/3 carrying the newer mostly red livery follows behind on the 49 service from Cannon Street to Crumpsall Green. The learner driver of No 3101 has the close company of an instructor standing in the half cab! Such an arrangement would hardly be tolerated today. Another official is on the upper deck, armed with pencil and clip board monitoring his progress. The building behind the Shell garage is the Timpson Shoe factory on the corner of Francis Street whilst the chimney in the far background is adjacent to the Boddington Brewery. One assumes that the driver won't be distracted by the imposing presence of H.M. Strangeways Prison which he is about to pass.

c1960 ● A. HAYNES COLLECTION

ROCHDALE ROAD

Rochdale Road looking North. A Crossley Mancunian is leaving the Collyhurst district and entering Harpurhey on route No 55 from Church Street to Nuthurst Road. The outward journey was by way of Conran Street and Moston Lane. This service was the first to be converted to trolleybus operation on the Moston routes, which came about on 4th November 1940. The bus will shortly pass the Essoldo cinema, seen behind the horse and cart in the background. The road then crosses over the 'Manchester Loop' line just before Queens Road junction.

1939 ● MANCHESTER CENTRAL LIBRARY

A new garage designed to accommodate 115 trolleybuses was officially declared open by the Lord Mayor on 1st March 1938. Rochdale Road Garage took an initial delivery of 76 vehicles divided equally between 4 and 6 wheelers. Nos 1000-27 were Crossley TDD4's with Metro Cammell/Crossley streamlined bodywork whilst Nos 1028-37 were Leyland TB4's with similar bodywork. The latter batches were Crossley TDD6's (1050-61) and Leyland TTB4's (1062-87), again with identical bodies. A number of these newly delivered vehicles seen inside the building have yet to be fitted with indicator blinds. The larger 6 wheel variety were considered unsuitable for the Moston routes because of the sharp corners encountered at Upper Conran Street/ Moston Lane and Thorp Road/Oldham Road junctions. The garage became a bus only base on 24th April 1956 leaving Hyde Road as the sole MCTD trolleybus operating garage.

1st MARCH 1938 ● A. HAYNES COLLECTION

The famous Manchester Streamline livery was introduced in late 1936 and many pre-war buses still sported it well into the post-war period - with slight variations. Although the first post-war deliveries had both the upper and lower deck window area, together with a band above the lower deck in cream, the first batch of 7' 6" Crossleys appeared with a streamlined swoop on the lower deck panels only. Daimler COG5 No **4261** (GNC 54) is in this condition seen passing C&A's store on Oldham Street. Behind the bus is Back Piccadilly, beyond which stand the shops of Peter Barrie (Costumiers) and Saxones (Shoes).

c.1948 ● THE OMNIBUS SOCIETY

OLDHAM STREET

A policeman on point duty ushers BUT Trolleybus No **1360** (ONE 760) round the corner from Oldham Road on to Great Ancoats Street on service No 213. The area, known as New Cross, is where Oldham Street meets its namesake road and Swan Street becomes Great Ancoats Street. The two prominent buildings are of architectural interest. St Paul's - Church of England, with its magnificent clock tower, no longer survives whereas the Crown and Kettle (formerly the Crown) was one of many bustling public houses on the northern fringes of the city centre. Apparently one of the rear rooms off the bar was wood panelled throughout, using timbers rescued from the R100 airship.

3rd APRIL 1959 ● P.J. THOMPSON

The futuristic Daily Express Building remains one of the most easily recognised buildings in the city - pure art deco with graceful curves and opulent styling. Having recently taken over from the tram, trolleybus No **1029** (DXJ 980), a Leyland TB4 with Metro Cammell/Crossley H28/26R streamline bodywork, is on its way down Great Ancoats Street from Stevenson Square to the Snipe, Audenshaw on service No 26. Both tram and trolleybus overhead wiring conspire to clutter the scene. The building immediately behind the trolleybus is a Manchester Corporation Electricity Department sub-station, which was provided to supply increased demand for the expanding network.

JULY 1938 ● A. HAYNES COLLECTION

CANNON STREET

During wartime, Manchester Corporation loaned out many of their buses to various operators. A typical example was Crosville Motor Services, who made use of a great number of Leyland TD1's in the Merseyside, Crewe and Wrexham areas. Upon return, many retained the letter L, applied by Crosville as a prefix to the fleet number for a short time. No **(L) 211** (VR 5766), now back working on its home patch, was away from October 1940 until February 1946 and survived in service for a further three years. There appears to be some consternation behind, where, judging by its jaunty angle, another bus seems to have mounted the kerb.

1946 ● R.C. JACKSON

Pre-war Leyland Titan TD5 No 3907 (FNF 807) swings into the bus station prior to working another 17X service, one of the many 'rush hour extras' as far as Middleton. She entered service in November 1939 as a streamliner but was soon carrying the red and grey wartime livery. Always a Queens Road vehicle, No 3907 saw out the 1950's before withdrawal, which came in October 1960. She was sold to R. Blair of Blackley whose firm were responsible for scrapping large numbers of Corporation vehicles. A great variety could be observed passing in and out of Cannon Street bus station by day. The North Western Road Car Company jointly operated the No 3 route to Flixton (Carrington Road) via Stretford and Urmston and both the Salford and Bury Corporations were represented on the No 35 service to Bury, which also ran in conjunction with Manchester. No overnight services operated from the terminus.

c.1958 ● JOHN FOZARD

Manchester's first post-war Leylands were a batch of 7'6" wide buses. PD1/1 No **3035** (GVR 237) is waiting to leave on the No 63 service between Cannon Street and Heywood. Running at 20 minute intervals, a time of 42 minutes was allowed for the journey down Rochdale Road, the main stages being at Queens Road, Blackley Tram Office, Middleton, Langley Lane and Hopwood. This order for 50 narrow vehicles was evenly split between Queens Road and Northenden depots, the latter making use of their quota on the 44/108 and 64 routes from Piccadilly to Baguley Sanitorium, Timperley and Ringway or Styal respectively - where narrow lanes were encountered en-route. Eight members (including No 3035) were transferred to Rochdale Road when that garage took its first delivery of motor buses.

c.1950 ● PAUL SHACKCLOTH COLLECTION

ROCHDALE CORPORATION

Streamline liveried vehicles continued to find favour post-war with Rochdale Corporation, long after Manchester had dispensed with theirs. No **247** (JDK 747) is a Daimler CVG6 with Weymann bodywork and built in 1953. The bulk of the fleet during the mid 1960's was made up of vehicles with AEC Regent chassis, again with Weymann bodies. The attractive lines are evident here on the vehicle waiting to work the jointly operated No 17 back to its home town. The colours were ivory and blue. Manchester Cathedral, a prominent landmark in the background, happily survived the German blitz at which time much was destroyed in the immediate vicinity.

1960 ● **DAVID YOUNG COLLECTION**

Cannon Street Bus Station offered little in the way of passenger comfort by way of shelter. Invariably a bus stood ready to leave, such was the frequency of most services from here. A pair of Queens Road Leyland Titan PD2/3's await departure. No **3256** (JND 657) on route No 26, is about to travel to Greengate, a destination not to be confused with Moston, Gardener's Arms - the same in this case! (Greengate usually signified a rush hour extra to Avro's bus park). After turning right into Victoria Street, the bus will then pass under Platform 11 Middle between Victoria and Exchange Stations, proceeding as far as Cheetham Hill via Great Ducie Street and Waterloo Road. Over the stone setts, facing the other direction and standing ready to turn into Corporation Street is No **3264** (JND 665) on the 17 - Rochdale service.

1953 ● **PAUL SHACKCLOTH COLLECTION**

OLDHAM CORPORATION

Another Jointly operated service into Cannon Street was the No 59, operating to Shaw, Wren's Nest. Unlike Rochdale, Oldham Corporation favoured Leyland Titan vehicles with Roe bodywork. A typical example is No **349** (EBU 879). Behind the bus stands Leyland Tiger **A88** (VR 5996), ex-fleet No 30 built in March 1930, which acted as a staff canteen here between 1950 and 1961. The Corn & Produce Exchange buildings in Hanging Ditch tower over the terminus. Many still fondly associate the Corn Exchange with the Manchester Model Railway Annual Exhibition, an event held just before the Christmas period, which featured those fabulous trams.

1958 ● **JOHN FOZARD**

CHURCH STREET

When trolleybus services Nos 32 & 33 were re-routed inward via Shude Hill and outward via Oldham Street in July 1941, Church Street became their city termini. (Stevenson Square had been used for a short period beforehand) It could hardly be described as a bus station, especially as the destination blinds showed High Street until 1953! Church Street was added to the list from that time but shortly afterwards the route was renumbered No 212/4. Trolleybus operation ceased on 24th April 1955 at which time the newly created motorbus service No 114 began operating from here to Moston (Ben Brierley). One of the surviving Leyland Titan PD1's, No **3030** (GVR 232) stands by the time clock awaiting departure.

JANUARY 1965 ● A. HAYNES COLLECTION

STEVENSON SQUARE

Rush hour in the Square brings vehicles of Crossley and Leyland origin together, working alongside on extras. Service No 98 between Stevenson Square and Waterhead was intensive throughout the day, offering a ten minute interval at worst but significantly augmented during the peak periods. Both buses are in the later, mostly red livery but Crossley DD42/4 No **2091** (GVR 185) still possesses a Maltese Cross on its radiator cowl. The majority of these vehicles had lost this symbol in favour of the 'Crossley' nameplate many years beforehand, a politically sensitive decision at the time. Behind this bus stands Leyland PD2/3 No **3215** (JND 616), which will work another shortened service to Hollinwood after an indicator change. Both buses were then based at Rochdale Road Garage.

1963 ● ABCROSS

A **brand new Metro-Cammell bodied** Leyland PD2/40 No **3534** (UNB 534) stands in the bus station. Whilst Piccadilly lay in the heart of city and dealt with a large proportion of the Corporation's transport services, Stevenson Square and Cannon Street Bus Stations were deliberately sited to the north to ease congestion. Lower Mosley Street was similarly placed on the south side. The Square was also home for 'soap box' style political rallies for many years, permitted by Authority on Sundays when they would cause little or no disruption to tram and bus services.

1958 ● JOHN FOZARD

MILES PLATTING INCLINE

Ivatt Class 2 2-6-0 No 46437 gets away, up the incline with a Divisional Engineer's Special. Although the rule book allowed for the coach to be propelled at 50mph, no lifeguards were fitted to this vehicle at either end! The crew were therefore instructed to proceed with caution around the Central Division (and beyond) at a gingerly rate.

23rd AUGUST 1966 ● TOM HEAVYSIDE

▶ **A Jubilee in full cry.** The classic lines of Stanier's renowned masterpiece are seen to great effect as she attacks the bank with a relief train to Leeds. This was to become a rare bird though. No **45673 Keppel** carries a painted code 10B - unusual for the period, and was a Preston loco from April 1951 until October 1952. She then took up residence at Perth (via Carlisle Kingmoor) in February 1953 before moving to Corkerhill (Glasgow) in June 1960 from where the loco was withdrawn. Keppel revisited the Manchester area at least once after the transfer north when her 63A shedplate was observed at Newton Heath on 19th July 1959, possibly having been borrowed by Polmadie. Also of interest are the leading coaches in this scratch set. The first is a North British Standard 3rd Class Corridor example whilst behind is a 60ft Midland period LMS Vestibule 3rd, 125 of which were built at Derby, several being converted as dining cars.

JULY 1951 ● ARTHUR BENDELL

The crew of ex-L&Y No 52207 will have given 'two crows' in response to the train engine's 'single crow', confirming their readiness to assist a passenger train for an assault on the Miles Platting Incline. This particular loco had a somewhat chequered career in that it was one of a select number which saw service as a works shunter at Crewe from September 1953 until November 1959 before returning to civvy street for a further 18 months' work. It went to Bury for a brief spell before ending its days at Lees, Oldham in May 1961.

3rd JUNE 1952 ● PAUL SHACKCLOTH COLLECTION

A view over the Irk Valley. Red Bank Carriage Sidings are in the distance beyond which are a series of 'walk up' flats, built by the Council in the 1950's to relieve the chronic housing shortage in the Cheetham area. A similar view in early L&Y days would have revealed Boardman's Brewery, which once stood overlooking the railway on the corner of Cheetham Street and Red Bank. They ceased brewing in 1905. Stanier Class 8F 2-8-0 No **48111** trundles up the bank in the first of a series of three photographs taken in the vicinity of Rochdale Road Gasworks.

26th AUGUST 1966 ● BRIAN CRAMER

The vicinity east of Victoria Station was rich in industrial heritage, offering many diverse activities. A metal foundry, glue and oilworks, saw mills and timber yards rubbed shoulders with the sprawling gasworks. Red Bank Spring & Axle Works, whose sign appears on many photos taken off the end of Platform 11, also occupied sites on either side of the loop line near Victoria East Junction signalbox. A filthy Stanier Class Five, whose cabside number **44982** has been wiped over for identification, drifts down the bank light engine en-route to Ordsall Lane. The Carlisle Kingmoor loco had recently been employed on inter-regional excursion duty and is still displaying the reporting number 1X51, chalked high on the smokebox door.

26th AUGUST 1966 ● BRIAN CRAMER

It was common practice towards the end of steam to withdraw a loco from service at the drop of a hat for the most trivial of reasons. One that the authorities overlooked was Ivatt Class 2 2-6-0 No **46406** which, although recorded on the enginemen's report cards, ran with a cracked chimney for some time. She is engaged in a spot of pilot work and is setting back parcels vans into the bays. The holding sidings for the EMU Bury line stock lay behind on the south side of the running lines within the shadow of Rochdale Road Gasworks.

26th AUGUST 1966 ● BRIAN CRAMER

OVERLEAF, TOP **Hauling a mixed bag of vestibuled and non-vestibuled ex-LNER stock,** Edge Hill Royal Scot 4-6-0 No **46111** *Royal Fusilier* hammers up the bank with an extra. Because of restricted clearance, balance weights were centrally sited on certain signal posts in the area. The Down Fast to the right of the loco illustrates the arrangement. They would normally be situated at ground level by the base of the post. The heavy exhaust from the Scot all but obliterates the upper quadrant signal arm in the off position controlling the Down Slow line.

AUGUST 1952 ● ARTHUR BENDELL

OVERLEAF, CENTRE **The combination of a 'Derby 4' piloting a Class Five or Jubilee** wasn't unusual on Summer Saturdays during the 1950's. The trains were often returning excursions bound for the Oldham area which would be routed via the O,A&GB line from the junction at Ashton. Both locos carry recently applied BR numbers although their tenders are inconsistent. Class 4F 0-6-0 No **44479** (24A - Accrington) has an adapted example for company, offering extra protection for the crew but still sporting the letters LMS whist the unidentified Stanier Class Five 4-6-0's tender carries the words British Railways. JULY 1951 ● ARTHUR BENDELL

OVERLEAF, BOTTOM **An all too common sight** on BR during the latter days were cavalcades of withdrawn locos bound for various scrap yards. The crew of an unidentified Stanier 8F 2-8-0 will welcome the assistance of Ivatt Class 2 2-6-0 No **46411**. Their train, comprising a trio of WD 2-8-0's, two buffer wagons and a brake van, is a combined weight of over 400 tons. 21st AUGUST 1964 ● R.S. GREENWOOD

Despite the opening of the Manchester Loop line in 1877, relieving the Miles Platting area of traffic directly bound for the Calder Valley, it was still necessary to quadruple the direct line. From April 1900, local trains concentrated on the southerly pair of tracks leading directly into the bay platforms at Victoria Station. These are in the left foreground. In addition, the electrified lines to Bury ran parallel at the foot of the incline before dropping away through Collyhurst Tunnel which passed directly under it at a point just north of Newtown No 2 signalbox. Stanier Class Five No **45206** forges up the bank with rear end assistance on the Down fast, hauling a relief train to Leeds.

JULY 1953 ● ARTHUR BENDELL

At classic locations such as this, the photographer would often rub shoulders (or sit on a crumbling brick wall at a high elevation in this case) with fellow enthusiasts recording video footage of the final months of steam. This particular occasion, a summer Saturday morning in 1967, is immortalised in the video *'Summer of 68'*. The benefits of back lighting, telephoto lens and a Stanier Class Five No **44817** working hard upgrade combine to produce this dramatic image. A Gloucester R.C.&W. motor parcels van stands alone within the former Newtown Carriage Sidings whilst two other steam locos are in evidence in the distance. The first, a Standard Class Five No **73039**, is offering banking assistance to the train bound for the east coast whilst passing an unidentified light engine further down the incline. **JULY 1967 ● BERNARD CRICK**

During the Summer timetable of 1953, the 9.30am MFO Manchester Exchange - Newcastle was worked as far as Leeds City by a Carlisle Upperby unrebuilt Patriot or Jubilee. The loco then returned on a South Shields - Manchester train later in the day. A member of the former class, 4-6-0 No **45505 *The Royal Army Ordnance Corps*** is half way up Miles Platting bank, without assistance, with a train made up of ex-LNER stock. Rapidly gaining ground on the Down slow line is Fairburn Class 4 2-6-4T No **42288** bound for its home depot, Newton Heath. Behind the train lie Newtown Carriage Sidings whilst to the right of the loco, the tower of Strangeways prison is prominent above the gasometer, a part of the Rochdale Road Gasworks complex.   **AUGUST 1953 ● ARTHUR BENDELL**

The daily morning service to Newcastle was regularly in the hands of Class 6/7P power provided by Edge Hill Depot. Here, one of the stud of Royal Scots allocated there, No **46149 *The Middlesex Regiment*** has accepted the assistance of a banking engine as far as Miles Platting Junction box where it will drop off. A Patricroft loco will have buffered up prior to departure at 9.51am from Exchange's Platform 5.

AUGUST 1953 ● ARTHUR BENDELL

Immaculate Permanent Way - a clean Jubilee in good mechanical order - a smart set of blood and custard stock - a loco working hard upgrade with safety valve blowing - the fireman in view as a bonus - all these elements have been carefully considered by that eminent photographer of the early 1950's - Arthur Bendell. Beyond his control, however, was the weather but this day his luck was in - the sun was shining. In common with many of his contemporaries, it would appear that Arthur rarely pressed the shutter in adverse conditions. He has positioned himself on New Allen Street bridge to record the passing of Stanier Jubilee 4-6-0 No **45635 *Tobago*** in the cutting approaching the summit of the incline. The banker has just burst clear of Osborne Street bridge whilst to the left, unfortunately out of view, were parts of the site of the former Manchester and Leeds Railway workshops and engine shed complex.   **AUGUST 1953 ● ARTHUR BENDELL**

A 'Jubilee' in trouble. Stanier 4-6-0 No **45642 *Boscawen*** was the original forerunner of the class, being built as 5552 and un-named. In exchange, newly built 5642 was re-numbered 5552 in April 1935 and named 'Silver Jubilee'. As a long standing resident of Newton Heath, the loco was considered by many enginemen there to be the 'black sheep' of the Jubilee family and prone to mechanical failure, possibly because of dubious prototype features. As a consequence it was frequently overlooked on the Glasgow turns but nevertheless, reached Scotland on a number of occasions. The depot's Cowans and Sheldon 50 ton crane is in attendance lifting 16 ton mineral wagons clear in order to gain access to the tender which has 'jumped' the rails. Miles Platting Junction Signalbox is just in view.

AUGUST 1964 ● BERNARD CRICK

MILES PLATTING SUMMIT

The 9.00am Liverpool Lime Street to Newcastle express comes off the Down Slow line with Edge Hill's immaculate Royal Scot No **46111** *Royal Fusilier* in charge. The train is passing Collyhurst Junction signalbox on time at 10.00am but is made up of an interesting variety of coaching stock. An unidentified ex-L&Y Class 3F Saddle Tank goes about it's business on the Collyhurst Street Shunt - Number 3 within the Miles Platting Shunt Engine links. The engine worked continuously from 6.05am Mondays Only to 6.00am Sundays Only.

5th AUGUST 1951 ● **ARTHUR BENDELL**

Unrebuilt Royal Scot Class 4-6-0 No 46156 *The South Wales Borderer* arrives at the summit of the bank with the same train. With the sanders hard on, speed will have reduced to about 20mph at this point, enabling the photographer to expose his film at the critical moment. A bonus is the presence of Fairburn 2-6-4T No **42285** awaiting the signal on the Down Slow line. Notice the gradient sign (1 in 49/57) in picture to the right whilst another unidentified loco passes overhead from Tank Yard towards New Allen Street Junction. This result had been achieved using a Super Ikonta 530/2 camera fitted with a Zeiss Tessar lens. Exposure time was 1/400 second at F8 under a hazy sun.

11th OCTOBER 1952 ● **ARTHUR BENDELL**

OLDHAM ROAD GOODS DEPOT

Oldham Road Station, terminus of the *Manchester and Leeds Railway,* opened on 4th July 1839 amidst scenes of great jubilation. Its life as a passenger station, however, was extremely short lived. The development of Victoria, a station more conveniently situated in the city also offered a direct connection with the *Manchester and Liverpool Railway* and opened just over four years later on 1st January 1844. From this date, Oldham Road became exclusively goods-orientated. Standing at the end of a 58-arch viaduct which extended from Collyhurst, the elevated platforms served hoists to lower wagons to ground level. The rapid development of goods handling facilities saw the introduction of a spur in 1874. This was a severe incline (1 in 27), worked under strict local instruction on the west side of the viaduct, offering a direct access into the sprawling yard which served a number of sheds. The largest of these was the 14-road Shipping and Delivery Shed, capable of handling up to 120 wagons at any one time. Fruit and provisions, cotton, cloth and general produce also had their own buildings. Additionally, a large grain warehouse stood near the Timekeepers and Inspectors Office at the depot entrance. Access to the nearby Rochdale Road Gas Works was also gained from the yard. The 23-acre site was situated between the main Rochdale and Oldham Roads, bound by the connecting Thompson Street. A substantial area between Oldham Road and the station buildings handled the immense potato traffic. The depot was the principal outlet in the North West and a wholesale potato market operated on the premises. The diminutive 'Pug' 0-4-0 saddle tanks worked the yard for many years, outstationed from Newton Heath from where coal was regularly delivered. They became known as the 'Potato' engines and many a spud was baked to perfection under the dome for a locoman's lunch. *Above:* Three modes of transport can be seen in the potato yard during this transitionary period. A heavily laden horse drawn cart rubs shoulders with a Scammell Scarab tractor whilst a pre-war motor lorry stands to the left. In L&Y days, over 250 horses were stabled under the arches here. The elevated train shed stands behind an assortment of fruit vans whilst the grain warehouse brings up the background behind the Scarab. *Below:* The original offices for the *Manchester and Leeds Railway* whose name and clock remained in situ throughout. The original booking office was at ground level. Note the wagon turntables and the track passing through the arch which led into the Shipping and Delivery Shed yard.   **AUGUST 1953 ● C.H.A. TOWNLEY**

Driver Billy Green concentrates on the yard shunter's hand signals, who is 'offering the distance' as his ex-L&Y Radial tank No **50850** buffers up to the coaching stock. The loco had taken water and would shortly depart with the 'Central Lancashire Railtour'. This was a particularly nostalgic trip for many as the popular 2-4-2 tanks had performed heroics in the area for many years. No 50850 was the last survivor of the class and had eked out her time at Southport Chapel Street on station pilot duties since February 1960, having been based at Bolton throughout the 1950's. She arrived light engine at Newton Heath on Friday 16th September in readiness for the trip, but on the Sunday was observed back on Bolton Shed on her way home. One wonders whether the Operating Department diverted her there for servicing or for old times sake.

17th SEPTEMBER 1960 ● IAN G. HOLT

CENTRAL LANCASHIRE RAILTOUR

A rare glimpse around the back of the original train shed. This was the first occasion that passengers had enjoyed the facility here for 116 years but the structure appears to be in sound condition. The railtour did not return to Oldham Road but terminated at Rochdale after travelling by way of Middleton Junction, Chadderton Goods, the Werneth Incline (supported by L&Y 0-6-0 No 52271), Castleton, Woolfold, Bury Bolton Street, Radcliffe North and West Junctions, Bradley Fold Junction, Bolton, Chorley, Feniscowles, Blackburn, Padiham, Copy Pit, Todmorden, Rochdale, Bury Loco Junction, Radcliffe Bridge, Clifton Junction, Manchester Victoria, Miles Platting, Hollinwood, Oldham and Rochdale. No 50850 then took the empty stock to Lightbowne Sidings, Newton Heath.

17th SEPTEMBER 1960 ● G. HARROP

OLDHAM ROAD, COLLYHURST STREET

Oldham Road was a thoroughfare of exuberant activity. Mile after mile of shops, terraced houses, mills, factories, theatres, chapels and churches, not to mention the numerous public houses. It was a densely populated area of predominantly working class people and this photograph nicely illustrates the everyday hustle and bustle. Traffic jostles for position awaiting the Collyhurst Street lights to change with Car No **876** taking its turn. It was built as one of a large batch by English Electric between December 1919 and July 1922 - the heyday of the Manchester tramcar. By 1939 only 450 cars remained in service and their days were numbered. The onset of war prolonged the agony and a few lasted long enough to run during the early days of British Railways. The last car made its farewell appearance on the south side of the city on 10th January 1949. A large public house called the 'White Hart Hotel' stood on the corner of Collyhurst Street and sold Chesters Ales, a local brewery renowned for its dark 'fighting' mild.

2nd AUGUST 1938 ● H.B. PRIESTLEY

The same location but differing routes and garages. Passing the Osborne Cinema on their way into the city on Sunday services are Leyland Titan PD1/3 No **3185** (JNA 486), a Queens Road bus engaged on the 54 service between Middleton and Stevenson Square. A few minutes later, working the cross-city No 65, a two year old Leyland PD2/12 No **3334** (NNB 174) passed by. The route from Moston, Gardener's Arms to Trafford Park (Third Avenue) was by way of New Moston, Newton Heath (with views of the depot from the upper deck), Piccadilly, All Saints and Old Trafford. All 40 examples of these models were based at Hyde Road at the time. *Happily, one of the class, No 3368 (NNB 208) has been secured for preservation.* The forlorn Osborne Cinema still appears to be open - before the war she was one of over a hundred 'picture houses' in and around the city. By 1965 less than forty remained.

20th MARCH 1955 ● **RAY DUNNING**

COLLYHURST JUNCTION

The site of the old Manchester & Leeds complex. The surviving part of the original locomotive and carriage works building and tower can be seen. This nearly outlived steam on BR, being demolished as late as 1966. The tracks to the left, part of the original M&L main line, led to Oldham Road Goods Station whilst the notorious Miles Platting incline is to the right. The bridge carrying the New Allen Street - Brewery Sidings line, constructed in 1889, resulted in much of the original works being swept away. A pair of ex-L&Y Saddletanks are visible, standing on land once occupied by the locomotive depot. That nearer is sandwiched between the coal stage and parachute water tank. These facilities enabled certain locos engaged on Miles Platting shunting diagrams to be stabled for lengthy periods, only returning to their depot for routine maintenance, boiler washouts etc. New Allen Street signal box stands at the junction in the distance.　　**MAY 1956** ● **C.H.A. TOWNLEY**

A Stockport (Tiviot Dale) to Morecambe excursion is about to make the regulation cautious descent of Miles Platting incline on a fine summer Saturday morning. This period, the early 1950's, is a time considered by many enthusiasts to be the halcyon days. The view, taken from the steps of Collyhurst Street signalbox, is full of interest. Immediately behind the retaining wall are the lines leading from Brewery Sidings to New Allen Street Junction beyond which lies a busy Tank Yard. The train has just negotiated Miles Platting Junction and amidst a sea of signals, but those in the foreground, at the end of the new bridge parapet, are pure L&Y vintage. The train is taking an unusual route. Rather than heading west out of Stockport and traversing the CLC, it has reached this point by way of Brinnington Junction, Reddish Junction, Ashburys, Midland Junction and Philips Park. The loco is a Gorton B1 4-6-0, No **61159** and with the passing time recorded as 10.50am, it will be well into the afternoon before arrival at Morecambe is effected.　　**5th AUGUST 1951** ● **ARTHUR BENDELL**

OLDHAM ROAD

One of the busiest junctions on Oldham Road was that with Hulme Hall Lane and Queens Road, more commonly known as 'Playhouse Corner'. A cyclist crosses in the Rochdale Road direction in front of English Electric Car No **1040** which stands at the tram stop and awaits the traffic lights. The car, one of the Nos 1004 - 1053 batch, had recently been transferred. When Queens Road became a 'bus only' garage in February 1938, the remaining cars and duties were transferred to Hyde Road in the short term. Service No 23 from Hollinwood to Chorlton had another 11 months before buses took over. A cross-section of society appears to be present. The conductor leans back against the window, allowing the workers, some clad in overalls, to clamber aboard. The management, the suited gentlemen with bowler hats, await their turn. Some will live locally whilst others may have transferred off a No 53 service which intersected here and was already bus operated. The bridge carrying the Ashton line over Oldham Road is in the background of this view looking towards Newton Heath.　**2nd AUGUST 1938 ● H.B. PRIESTLEY**

PLAYHOUSE CORNER

On 2nd July 1939, just before the outbreak of World War Two, bus service No 82 took over from tram No 23 on the cross-city route between Chorlton and Hollinwood. Leyland Titan PD1/3 No **3079** (GVR 281) has the green light and crosses Hulme Hall Lane on the north - south route which had reverted to a Queens Road duty. Meanwhile, travelling in the opposite direction, a laden truck of river sand owned by Coopers looks suspiciously back heavy. Behind is a maroon BR enamel sign affixed to a lamp standard offering directions to the nearby Miles Platting Station. The local branch of Williams Deacons Bank stands on the corner of Queens Road whilst on the opposite side stood the 'Playhouse Cinema', a well respected establishment with comfortable seating which once boasted of having a billiards room in the basement.

10th JUNE 1955 ● RAY DUNNING

MILES PLATTING STATION

An old fashioned Manchester pea souper. During the days of steam, fogs were common during the winter months, especially in and around the city where countless coal fires emitted smoke which only compounded the problem. A Permanent Way Gang carry on regardless as an unidentified Class Five creeps by off the Ashton line. The men are busily engaged in tightening coach screws on chairs with the appropriate spanner. Such practices would hardly be tolerated by the Health and Safety Inspectorate of today although their activities are under the constant supervision of signalmen in the nearby Miles Platting Junction signalbox. The bracket signals themselves are worthy of mention. That on the left controlling the route from Thorpes Bridge Junction is of standard LMS pattern with broad flange beam bracket, whilst its neighbour is of L&Y origin, modified with upper quadrant arms.   **12th APRIL 1957 ● H.C. CASSERLEY**

The austere entrance to Miles Platting Station. Serious cracks have appeared in the brickwork here, a consequence of the multitude of traffic on both Queens Road and the railway overbridges over many years. A pedestrian shows passing interest in a Class Five coming off the Ashton branch whilst the advert is of great significance. The end of steam coincided with the national promotion of 'keg' beers. Youngers 'Tartan' and Watneys 'Red Barrel' were two of the flagship products which became widely available. The campaign immediately brought pressure to bear on the independent brewers, the local Wilsons Brewery becoming an early casualty. The eventual outcome was the creation of the CAMRA organisation in 1972, who successfully arrested the trend.

1968 ● JOHN G. HARTSHONE COLLECTION

One of the busiest signalboxes on the region and, indeed, in the country, was Miles Platting Junction. Bill Hodges worked here for a great number of years.   **3rd AUGUST 1967 ● R.S. GREENWOOD**

Fireman Geoff Popplewell is on the footplate of Hughes Crab 2-6-0 No **42705** proceeding light engine through Platform 1 at Miles Platting Station and on towards its home depot. This pleasing study is of one of the most versatile classes of loco which worked during LMS and BR days. Introduced in 1926 by Hughes but built under the direction of Fowler, the popular 'Crabs' were the veritable 'maids of all work', ideally suited to cover many of Newton Heath's diverse range of duties. The splitting signal by the box is fitted for dual usage because of restrictions in the area and is now happily preserved at the Brookside Garden Centre, Poynton, alongside other items of railway memorabilia. Geoff later accepted a more senior post across the city on the 'Wessie' at Longsight.

1st MAY 1959 ● R. KEELEY

A view of the island platform from a passing train bound for Stalybridge. The original station (M&L) opened here on 1st January 1844 with the commencement of local services to Manchester Victoria. The Ashton branch (from Miles Platting to Ashton Charlestown) was completed in April 1846 resulting in the development of additional Up and Down platforms. The half glazed subway entrance rises from the left whilst the canopy reveals an open expanse of platform. The staff have taken the opportunity to introduce circular rockeries which seems somewhat out of character for the area. Just out of view to the right stood a goods office, a large two-storey building which acted as headquarters for the Area Manager and his senior goods agents.

1st JUNE 1968 ● J.P. ALSOP

A 'Super D' 0-8-0 No 49377 forges through The Up Platform off the Ashton branch showing Class 'H' through freight lamps. She will shortly be brought to a standstill before Collyhurst Street box whilst the fireman pins down the wagon brakes for the descent of Miles Platting bank. Behind the timber waiting room were the Up and Down east goods avoiding lines from Philips Park. A local instruction was an embargo on freight traffic through the busy Victoria Station between the hours of 7.25am and 10.00am daily, 3.30pm - 6.30pm Saturdays excepted and from 11.45am until 1.45pm on Saturdays only. This usually resulted in a number of trains being held in various sections in the area. The ruling was strictly enforced by the Main Line Inspector at Victoria East Junction with the exception of engines and brake vans or by special dispensation (for example, a breakdown train). **1st MAY 1959 ● R. KEELEY**

Ex-L&Y 2-4-2T No 50644 come off the spur connecting the Ashton Branch with the original Manchester and Leeds line north of Miles Platting station, known to railwaymen as 'India Rubber Junction'. The ex-LMS lattice post bracket signal is of interest. Due to the restricted space between the Down running line and the adjacent sidings, the balance lever operating mechanism had to be located at a high level. This in turn required an additional ladder for maintenance, which can be seen to the right of the post. Attached to this main post is a plate with a hole in it. This is a vitreous enamel sign indicating the presence of a 'fireman's call box' to the train crew. The device itself was located at the signal and required the Driver or Fireman to press a plunger if their train had been held at the signal for more than two minutes. This actuated a bell/buzzer or indicator in Brewery Sidings signalbox to remind the signalman of the presence of the train. In normal situations this avoided the need for a member of the train crew to go to the box and carry out the provision of Rule 55 to verbally remind the signalman of the train's presence. Alternatively, another more common form of Rule 55 exemption was a track circuit which was signified by a diamond sign on the signal post. **26th JULY 1953 ● ARTHUR BENDELL**

Fine views of a journey could be obtained from the leading compartment of a Diesel Multiple Unit. A train bound for Oldham and Rochdale has just left Miles Platting Station and is rapidly overtaking a Stanier Class Five heading for the shed on the Down Slow line. Thorpes Bridge and the coal hopper are away down the line, whilst the new distribution warehouse of Wilsons Brewery, utilising pre-cast concrete unit roof sections, stands to the left. Part of the original Newton Heath Carriage Works building is behind the loco. The large wheel in the driver's cab is the handbrake and to its left is the emergency application vacuum brake. **26th MAY 1967 ● PAUL SHACKCLOTH**

MATTHEW SWAIN'S SIDING

The ironfounders Matthew Swain Ltd were founded in 1878 and had premises bound by Albatross Street and Holt Street just off the Oldham Road. The land extended to the Manchester and Leeds main line on the Up side at a point half a mile north of Miles Platting Station. For many years a mainstay of their production was cast iron hollow ware which included large cooking pots. These were known as 'Negro Pots' and were the type familiar in many cartoons of the time which usually featured unfortunate, misguided missionaries. Photographic evidence suggests prodigious quantities of hollow ware bound for the West Indies and Africa began their journey by rail in customised, specially adapted vans supplied by the Lancashire and Yorkshire Railway Company from the outset. The likely destination of the trains would be Liverpool dockside. Production began to diversify between the wars and although the Company were still producing small quantities of export hollow ware into the early 1960's, they eventually ceased trading in 1980.

ABOVE **Standing at the head of a train** of private owner vans in Brewery Sidings is 0-6-0 Saddle Tank No **172**. This locomotive was built by Kitsons for the L&YR as an 0-6-0 tender engine in November 1878 and was converted to a Saddle Tank in October 1892. She was withdrawn in June 1927 without ever receiving her allotted LMS number (11339). The train carried the message 'SHIPMENT OF NEGRO POTS' with two characters per van. The Newton Heath Driver and Fireman stand alongside their loco whilst the Guard and Yardman complete with shunting pole pose for what may have been an official company photograph   **c.1908 ● PAUL JORDAN COLLECTION**

BELOW **Access to the private sidings** was from a spur off the Up line between Thorpes Bridge Junction and Brewery Sidings. A pronounced incline is evident and local instructions stated that *'under no circumstances must wagons be detached into these sidings without first being spragged, and vehicles with a wheelbase of more than 10 feet must not pass over the curve leading to the loading shed'*. Another rebuilt Saddle Tank, No **245** stands in the siding with vans. This loco was built just down the line at Miles Platting Works in May 1879 - she was similarly converted in March 1893 but lasted slightly longer in service. Her withdrawal coincided with the outbreak of war in May 1939 after carrying LMS number 11347.   **c.1908 ● PAUL JORDAN COLLECTION**

A view inside the loading shed showing several stacks of pots ready for dispatch. Matthew Swain's fleet of private owner wagons were supplemented by those of standard L&Y origin. A sliding roof offering easier access is evident here. The private siding closed in the late 1950's and an old battered wooden gate - originally positioned to protect the main line - survived to remind the passer by of a long lost industry.

c.1908 ● PAUL JORDAN COLLECTION

In 1953, Newton Heath Shed had to provide as many as 20 locos on a weekday for various local shunting duties. They were classified as 'Miles Platting Shunting Engines' and duties concerning Swain's Sidings were as follows:

No 1. BREWERY SIDINGS SHUNT
Newton Heath Class 3F (LY 0-6-0)
5.50am MO to 2.00pm SO continuous.
Works following trips:

	DAILY	
	Arrive am	Depart am
Brewery Sidings	-	9.05
Matthew Swain's Siding	9.10	9.20 LE
Brewery Sidings	9.23	
	pm	pm SX
Brewery Sidings	-	2.50
Matthew Swain's Siding	2.55	3.05
Brewery Sidings	3.08	
	DAILY	
Brewery Sidings	-	3.35 LE
Matthew Swain's Siding	3.40	4.00
Brewery Sidings	4.10	

The once proud Wilsons Brewery overlooks its namesake sidings and Class Five 4-6-0 No **44947** from Bolton shed bringing a mixed freight from the Thorpes Bridge Junction direction. Brewery Sidings signalbox lies in view on the east side of the Up main line beyond Miles Platting North Junction.

16th MAY 1968 ● PAUL SHACKCLOTH

A most unprecedented visitor to the Miles Platting area was this former GWR AEC railcar No **W4W** en-route from Hellifield (where it had been held in store with other preserved locos) to Swindon. It's slender lines were captured from a passing train but the railcar, sandwiched between a pair of 'flats', will soon be on the move south after a crew change behind Stanier Class 8F 2-8-0 No 48157.

23rd FEBRUARY 1967 ● R.S. GREENWOOD

BREWERY SIDINGS

PHILIPS PARK

The Manchester and District Railtour, organised by the RCTS, intended to cover as many of the lines and branches in the Greater Manchester area as possible which had either already lost their services or were under threat of closure. Certain routes planned by the society had not been sanctioned by Authority but the organisers had a contingency plan of routes in the Bolton area! In the event the itinerary was adhered to although it ran late from the outset due to engineering problems in the London Road station area. Ex-L&Y 2-4-2T No **50644** is passing Philips Park No 2 signalbox shortly after departure, having already traversed the Ardwick Junction - Midland Junction chord.

26th JULY 1953 ● C.H.A. TOWNLEY

The Newton Heath breakdown crane and attendant riding and tool van is called upon to assist the Miles Platting Signal and Telegraph gang. The work involved the recovery of a former L&Y wooden post bracket signal which had been converted to upper quadrant arms in LMS days. Its replacement in the foreground is a standard tubular steel version which is 'waiting to be dressed'. The signal arms, lamps, ladder, handrails and wire connections would be installed and a temporary ladder is in place for this purpose once the original signal had been removed. The old wooden post, made from pitch pine, would be sawn up with a cross-cut saw and no doubt would have ended up as firewood. This type of work was normally undertaken on a Sunday when traffic was light and may well have represented a nice spot of overtime for the breakdown gang crew - and not too far from home either!

c.1952 ● ARTHUR BENDELL

A loco which was in great demand for railtours was this member of the popular Fowler 2-6-4 tank class. No **42343** had been the choice of the Manchester University Railway Society for their 'Staffordshire Potter' railtour on 13th March 1965, previous to which she had enjoyed an outing to Leicestershire covering various obscure branches on 8th September 1962 - courtesy of the Manchester and Stephenson Locomotive Societies. Having been Stockport Edgeley's flagship engine (until the arrival of Bahamas), it came as a surprise to learn of its impending transfer to Springs Branch, Wigan in May 1965. No 42343 was on 8F's books (although she carried no shed-plate) when caught taking water at Philips Park whilst working a brake van tour, organised by the Locomotive Club of Great Britain (LCGB). This encompassed the Middleton Branch, scheduled for closure on 11th October 1965 and other lines in the North Manchester area.

7th AUGUST 1965 ● P. HUTCHINSON

STUART STREET POWER STATION

Stuart Street Power Station near Bradford Colliery was rail connected and utilised industrial locomotives owned by the CEGB. Access from the main line between Park and Clayton Bridge was gained at a point near Baguley Fold Junction on the Up side. A spur leading to Manchester Corporation Sidings facilitated the interchange of traffic. A single (and double in places) branch extended 980 yards, crossing the Medlock Valley by viaduct in the process, to the Power Station. Hudswell Clark 0-4-0 Saddletank No **1627** shunts wagons of ash brought from the boilers of the station. A ramshackle grab crane, just in view behind the mound, was used for unloading purposes. The main line can also be seen directly behind the engine.

1968 ● BERNARD CRICK

With the driver leaning from his cab, No **1672** trundles back to Stuart Street. The cooling towers which dominate the scene, were constructed in 1934 as part of the Power Station's rebuilding programme. Up to this time the branch delivered coal but an underground conveyor belt was installed from nearby Bradford Colliery offering a direct supply. The Station lasted a further ten years after the demise of steam on BR but the saddletank happily survives in preservation on the Tanfield Railway, Tyne and Wear. **1968 ● BERNARD CRICK**

The
locomotive
worksplate

PAUL JORDAN

BAGULEY FOLD JUNCTION

Stanier Class Five 4-6-0 No 44913 (8H - Birkenhead) passes the interchange sidings with a Manchester bound excursion. The splitting signal is for Philips Park East Junction, immediately beyond Park Station, which offered a direct connection off the main line towards Midland Junction.

AUGUST 1967 ● PAUL JORDAN

One of Stockport (Edgeley's) stud of Stanier Class Fives, No **45046,** is in charge of a Moston Exchange Sidings to Adswood express freight working. The location is between Park and Clayton Bridge stations and the land falling away in the foreground is part of the rubbish strewn Clayton Vale, later to be developed into a country park. Overlooking the line in the background is the 'Little Sisters of the Poor', known locally as the 'Nunnery'. From its inception in 1879, the Catholic order carried out much needed work in the Parish in conjunction with the local church and school. The home closed in 1972.

MARCH 1968 ● ERIC HUMPHREY

An **early period view** looking towards Stalybridge. An unidentified loco of LNWR origin has almost reached the level crossing with a Leeds New to Manchester Exchange express. From Stalybridge and into the city, the train was operating by arrangement with the L&Y who granted running powers to the London and North Western Railway Company. A running loop on the Up side immediately north of the station can be seen trailing in to the right of the engine. The L&Y poster under the station sign is a timetable of services, whilst the only word discernable on that at the far end of the platform is 'Belgium'. This would no doubt be in reference to the shipping service provided by the Company from the port of Goole. Otherwise the scene here has changed little over the years *(see below)*.

c.1910 ● JOHN RYAN COLLECTION

It was somewhat surprising that Stanier Class Five 4-6-0 No **44949** did not take up residence at either Lostock Hall or Carnforth with sister engines 44735 and 44809 when Newton Heath finally closed its doors to steam on 1st July 1968. It had been considered among the shed's remaining Class Fives as the most mechanically sound and received cosmetic attention from shed staff and enthusiasts alike as a consequence. Immaculately turned out in lined black livery, it hauled a number of railtours during the final months of steam. One such duty was a *'Stephenson Locomotive Society'* special organised by the Midland Area. The train ran from Birmingham to Ravenglass with the Class Five coming on at Stockport. From there it ran by way of Droylsden Junction, Manchester Victoria, Bolton and Blackburn to Carnforth.

26th MAY 1968 ● T.A. FLETCHER

Clayton Bridge Station, originally known as Culcheth Station, was opened by the Manchester and Leeds Railway on 13th April 1846. The nameboards changed in style over the years but this was the final example. The BR authorities made use of Gill Sans as their corporate type face and the bold version is seen here on the familiar vitreous enamel maroon background. The station remained gas lit until closure, which came just after the end of steam on 7th October 1968.

21st JUNE 1966 ● PAUL JORDAN

CLAYTON BRIDGE

The signal box was of East Lancashire origin, built by Smith and Yardley in YS Type 1 brick and opening in 1873. It became L&Y No 256 and the frame held 19 working levers with three spare. The signalman also controlled the adjacent level crossing, which was the only example within the Manchester area where a main running line crossed the road on the level. A small window in the rear of the cabin offered a view up Berry Brow of oncoming traffic.

29th JUNE 1965 ● R.S. GREENWOOD

Stanier 8F 2-8-0 No 48636 is held at the gates whilst the crew look anxiously on and appear to be eager to get away. The road crosses the line half way down a steep hill and was particularly hazardous during the frosts of winter. An additional problem was that uphill traffic was confronted with a blind corner immediately before the crossing. Lifting barriers were installed after the days of steam in early 1973 which caused a local public outcry. The signal box closed later during the same year (after surviving exactly 100 years) but the barriers were operated from the nearby Baguley Fold Junction box by CCTV.

21st JUNE 1966 ● PAUL JORDAN

Royal Scot 4-6-0 No 46155 *The Lancer* has drifted past the Up home signal and is brought to a stand immediately opposite the box. The engine, showing express headlamps, is in deplorable condition and may well be substituting for a failed diesel locomotive. A Pilotman, wearing the regulatory red armlet on the left arm above the elbow, has left the footplate to speak to the signalman, possibly with regard to permission for the train to enter section.

1964 ● PAUL JORDAN

One of Stockport Edgeley's Class Fives, No 45027 makes good progress through Clayton Bridge with an empty wagon train towards Droylsden Junction. It is passing over 'ten arches' - the Medlock viaduct spanning valley and river. Something of a mystery surrounds this photograph as the fireman appears to be waving a lamp from the footplate for no apparent reason - it was not for the benefit of the photographer!

MAY 1967 ● PAUL JORDAN

Once clear of the viaduct, the line passes through the pleasantly rural vicinity of Droylsden, between the eastern suburbs of Manchester and the more industrial Ashton and Stalybridge area. An unidentified Patricroft Standard Caprotti Class Five is in charge of an excursion heading for Scarborough.

AUGUST 1967 ● PAUL JORDAN

Leyland Titan PD2/40 No 3542 (UNB 542) on service 83 gets away up the hill from its Clayton Bridge Terminus by Andrew's Brow. Manchester Corporation took delivery of large numbers of these vehicles in 1958 which came with Metro-Cammell Orion Style bodywork. The 40-minute journey to Firswood, Cromwell Road was by way of North Road, Piccadilly, All Saints and Trafford Bar and operated out of Hyde Road Garage. The Medlock viaduct can be seen behind the towering electricity pylons.

6th JULY 1968 ● P.J. THOMPSON

DROYLSDEN

Trip workings around the Greater Manchester area involved large numbers of Newton Heath locos and men. Stanier 8F 2-8-0 No **48720** is working from Ashton Moss to Brindle Heath with a typical mixed bag of wagons.

30th JUNE 1960 ⬤
J. DAVENPORT

A returning inter-regional special from Blackpool North to Leeds City approaches Droylsden Junction with Stanier Jubilee Class 6P 4-6-0 No **45562** *Alberta* in charge. Such excursions would normally have travelled over Copy Pit, via Todmorden, Rose Grove and Blackburn, approaching Preston by way of Farrington Curve Junction. The detour via Manchester in this case may well have been primarily to serve the residents of the Huddersfield and Dewsbury areas. By this time *Alberta* was becoming one of the remaining 'high profile' members of the class, working out of Leeds Holbeck depot. The stud of Jubilees were kept in clean condition by a handful of dedicated enthusiasts who made regular pilgrimages to the depot.

2nd OCTOBER 1966 ⬤ T.A. FLETCHER

The 11.15am Newcastle to Llandudno express near Droylsden behind unrebuilt Patriot 4-6-0 No **45542**. The engine was based at Preston (24K) Shed and was one of only 10 within a class of 52 locos which remained un-named. She would probably have relieved an ex-LNER locomotive at Leeds City although the crew on the footplate would be either Farnley Junction or Patricroft men. They had route knowledge between Leeds and Manchester, then onwards to Chester General and beyond to the North Wales Coast.

30th JUNE 1960 ⬤
J. DAVENPORT

APPROACHING RED BANK

The 3.28pm Manchester Victoria to Bradford and Leeds (ex-2.30pm Liverpool Exchange) gets steadily away from East Junction behind an unidentified Low Moor Class Five. The ten coach train, on the Down Fast line, is approaching Footbridge Signalbox and Red Bank Carriage Sidings. Behind the box were loco servicing facilities including an electrically operated turntable - the only one of its kind in the Victoria area. An unidentified loco can be glimpsed on this table to the right of the parachute water tank. After a continuous climb through the northern suburbs of Newton Heath, Moston and Middleton Junction, the first stop is Rochdale, some 14 minutes after departure, then Littleborough, Todmorden, Hebden Bridge, Sowerby Bridge, Halifax and Low Moor where the train split. The leading five coaches continued to Bradford Exchange (arr. 4.30pm) whilst the rear portion went to Leeds Central (arr. 4.51pm).   **30th JUNE 1960 ● R.S. GREENWOOD**

The balanced multiple junction signal for the Down Slow line at the entrance to Red Bank Carriage Sidings. The arms from left to right represent: Down Slow to Down Fast Home and Cheetham Hill Distant, Down Slow Home and Cheetham Hill Distant, and Down Slow to Red Bank reception road. The short post is attached to the side of the viaduct and a number of guy ropes offer extra stability. Beyond the gasworks and the Irk valley is the Miles Platting incline with Newtown No 1 signalbox prominent.

30th JUNE 1960 ● R.S. GREENWOOD

The BR Standard Class 5MT 4-6-0 was a development of the highly successful Stanier version. Introduced in 1951, a batch of five (Nos 73025-29) went new to Blackpool Central shed in November/December but didn't last long there. Major inter-regional transfers re-directed them to ex-GWR depots Shrewsbury and Bristol, St Philips Marsh. No 73027 moved on to Swindon (via S.P.M.) in July 1954 where it stayed until February 1964 at which time it became the first of its class to be withdrawn. It was cut up at Swindon Works two months later. One of its regular duties was a stopping passenger to Manchester Victoria and return. No 73027, still awaiting a 24E shedplate, is leaving Red Bank with empty stock.

AUGUST 1952 ● **F. CONSTERDINE**

RED BANK CARRIAGE SIDINGS

The celebrated Heaton - Red Bank empty newspaper vans was renowned for producing unusual combinations of locomotives. The tradition was maintained until the very end when, on the last day of rostered steam working - a Sunday, the locos were none other than a pair of Stockport (Edgeley) engines with Britannia Pacific 4-6-2 No **70015 *Apollo*** piloting Stanier Class Five **No 45200.** They have just arrived and are awaiting instruction before setting the stock back into No 1 road (the longest road) at Cheetham Hill. The locos would then depart in tandem, tender first to Newton Heath which was a finishing turn for the crews - and the engines in this case. On weekdays they were both diagrammed to return to Yorkshire later in the evening on parcels trains, the pilot on the Burscough - Normanton and the train engine on the Victoria - York.

3rd JULY 1966 ● **M.K. LEWIS**

The smaller BR Standard Class 4MT 4-6-0's were designed at Brighton and built at Swindon for secondary services, primarily to replace the ageing 2P 4-4-0's. No 75019 was the last of a batch of five (75015-19) delivered new to Southport shed in March 1952. Unlike the larger Class Fives at Blackpool *(see above)*, these locos worked from the Lancashire coast town for over ten years before going their separate ways during 1963. They were ideal motive power for the Southport to Victoria stopping trains via Wigan Wallgate and were almost daily visitors to the city before the inevitable DMUs muscled in. No 75019 had a longer life than most of the 80 strong class, surviving until the end of steam, being withdrawn from Carnforth in August 1968. She is about to leave the carriage sidings with empty stock for Victoria Station.

AUGUST 1952 ● **F. CONSTERDINE**

This fine panoramic view offers a mixture of old and new as two Newton Heath locos are usefully employed on marshalling stock in Red Bank Carriage Sidings. The exhaust from Ivatt 2MT No **46448** partially obliterates the city's ever changing skyscape. Manchester Cathedral, above the loco, would have been the prominent feature in years gone by but now lies in the shadows of the many high rise office blocks. In the foreground, Stanier Class Five No **44893** stands coupled to brake and Royal Mail vans. The driver awaits the return of his fireman who has perhaps coupled them together. A four-car Cravens diesel multiple unit is stabled on the innermost through siding. This was the longest of seven and capable of stabling up to 14 bogies. By 1967 DMU's were making serious inroads into the traditional locomotive hauled passenger stock and rarely were these roads filled to capacity. A further 13 'dead end' sidings were available, all of which are visible and the majority are occupied by an assortment of coaches and parcels vans.   **22nd MARCH 1967** ● **ERIC BENTLEY**

Cheetham Hill Junction Signalbox was a standard L&Y pattern brick base, built in 1890 and measuring 36ft x 12ft. In 1918 the box had 64 levers with 8 spare. In addition, a two lever ground frame was installed in 1906 between Footbridge and Cheetham Hill boxes on the east side of the running lines. This served to control movements at the throat of Red Bank carriage sidings.

c.1968 ● **ALLAN SOMMERFIELD**

CHEETHAM HILL JUNCTION

Increasing congestion in the Miles Platting area resulted in the construction of a four track 'loop' between Victoria East Junction and Thorpes Bridge Junction, which opened on 29th October 1877. Most of the original line was through cutting or on viaduct but Red Bank and Cheetham Hill Carriage Sidings were developed after part of the cutting had been opened out on the south side in the early 1880's. The substantial footbridge in the distance connected North Street brickworks with Collyhurst Road and was known locally as '99 steps'. The track on the left is the throat of Cheetham Hill Carriage shed which opened in September 1884. In BR days number seven road regularly held the stock for the morning 'Glasgow'. The passing train is again the 'Newcastle' which has unassisted Jubilee 4-6-0 No **45717 Dauntless** for power. **MAY 1952** ● **ARTHUR BENDELL**

Jubilee 4-6-0 No 45661 Vernon gets into its stride with the 3N32 Red Bank - York ECS. The gradient from here to Thorpes Bridge Junction was formidable at 1 in 63 but still favourable to the Miles Platting incline (1 in 47) and a banking loco is in evidence. This is Southport's No **44687**, a Caprotti Class Five which will have arrived at Manchester Victoria Station earlier in the morning with a train from its home town. Having deposited empty carriages, the loco is free to offer assistance whilst en-route to Newton Heath shed for servicing. **23rd SEPTEMBER 1963** ● **ERIC BENTLEY**

A period scene rich in detail. The driver of Midland Railway Johnson 4-4-0 No **1659** admires the presence of an unidentified L&Y 'Highflyer' 4-4-2 drawing empty stock out of Queens Road Sidings, fully lined out in L&Y black livery. Both locos gleaming in the afternoon sunshine no doubt created a colourful spectacle for the photographer. The elegant Midland red loco was one of a batch (Nos 1657-66) delivered new to Newton Heath Depot in 1883 by arrangement with the L&Y to work the Hellifield services. She stands coupled to stock including a distinctive clerestory coach just clear of Cheetham Hill Carriage Shed. Just discernable in the left background is another L&Y loco, a 2-4-2T working bunker first towards Victoria on the Bury line. Note the various advertisements on the wooden carriage shed whilst duplicate signs strictly forbidding the entrance of locos look down over the carriage stalls.

28th JULY 1905 ● JOHN RYAN COLLECTION

This comparison nearly 60 years later reveals interesting changes. Missing are the adverts and signs adorning the carriage shed. Gone too are the dominating semaphores and the rather quaint gas lamp at the throat of Queens Road Carriage Sidings. A Metropolitan Cammell DMU now occupies the shed whilst a Class 504 EMU makes for Woodlands Road on the Bury line and the simple boundary fencing has been replaced by one of a more durable quality. The 4-6-0 Jubilee is none other than the celebrated No **45596 Bahamas**, the pride and joy of Stockport Edgeley shed, fitted with double chimney. She is reversing on to empty stock to form one of the many residential trains which left from here and Cheetham Hill from the mid afternoon.

15th MAY 1964 ● R.S. GREENWOOD

Twenty minutes later and it's time for No **45596 Bahamas** to draw forward. The DMU has departed in the meantime leaving no fewer than four Class Fives awaiting their turn to follow into Victoria Station.

15th MAY 1964 ● R.S. GREENWOOD

CARRIAGE WARMING DUTIES - CHEETHAM HILL

Three examples of the various withdrawn locomotives that acted as stationary boilers, warming the empty stock which stood within the six road Cheetham Hill Carriage Shed. Unfortunately many had both numbers and worksplates removed, rendering them anonymous.

Above: An early Barton Wright 0-4-4, believed to be ex-L&Y No **636.**   **2nd JULY 1961 ● C. APPLETON**
Below Left: An unidentified boiler seemingly mounted on an old tender frame.   **8th MAY 1960 ● R.S. GREENWOOD**
Below Right: Ex-LMS 3F 0-6-0 No **47564** with cab, tanks and rods removed, having been modified and re-numbered 2022 at Darlington Works. Withdrawn from Lostock Hall in March 1965, she arrived at Cheetham Hill in June 1966, remaining until 1970 at which time the loco was secured for preservation by the Midland Railway Centre.   **MARCH 1968 ● PAUL SHACKCLOTH**

OVERLEAF, TOP **A locomotive normally associated with the rival ex-LNWR route,** Stanier Jubilee 4-6-0 No **45695 *Minotaur*** crosses Smedley Viaduct at 11.35am with the morning Newcastle express. She was on Bank Hall's books for just six months between April and October 1952 having arrived from Blackpool and this would have been one of her last duties working out of the Merseyside depot. As a Farnley Junction engine she remained a regular sight in the Manchester area for a further decade.   **29th OCTOBER 1952 ● ARTHUR BENDELL**

OVERLEAF, CENTRE **An unusual combination on the Down Slow line** sees Ivatt Class 2 2-6-0 No **46414** piloting an unidentified Class Five with a returning excursion from Llandudno to the Oldham area. The Ivatt, still showing LMS on the tender, was probably attached at Manchester Exchange Station with the Western Lines reporting number board W520 being transferred from the train engine. They may well be travelling by way of the Hollinwood branch on this last leg of the journey.   **JULY 1951 ● ARTHUR BENDELL**

Smedley Junction Signalbox was bolted on to the girder bridge, supported by a wooden frame directly over the River Irk. It had a 48 lever frame (16 spare) and apparently the whole structure badly vibrated with the passage of a train. The box witnessed a head-on collision on 15th October 1959 between a Stanier Class Five No 45101, travelling light engine on the Up Fast, and a two-car Cravens Diesel Multiple Unit coming off the Irk Valley Chord on the 4.05pm Manchester Victoria to Rochdale. Fortunately both drivers had time to brake and reduce speed before impact, which was not severe. The accident report concluded that the direct cause was mischievous interference with signal equipment, probably by children.   **JUNE 1968 ● ALLAN SOMMERFIELD**

OVERLEAF, BOTTOM   **The Leeds/Bradford expresses from Liverpool** were often in the hands of Stanier Class Fives working out of Low Moor and Bank Hall Depots, but on this occasion No **45227** (27A) has control of the premier working - the Newcastle train. Smedley Junction is in the foreground and the fork to Irk Valley Junction, which offered a connection with the electrified Bury route, rises sharply to the left.   **MARCH 1951 ● ARTHUR BENDELL**

SMEDLEY JUNCTION

QUEENS ROAD CARRIAGE SIDINGS

Another view of *Bahamas* with a pair of Class Fives within the sidings. The lines in the foreground form the little used chord connecting Cheetham Hill Junction with Queens Road Junction. In the background, beyond the Bury electric line, is Smedley Road School.
15th MAY 1964 ● R.S. GREENWOOD

Relics of a bygone age. The Queens Road and Cheetham Hill area played host to a number of interesting veterans which acted as stationary steam heating boilers for the empty stock. This pair of Barton Wright 0-4-4's, built by Sharp Stewart in 1885/6 originally carried the Lancashire and Yorkshire Railway numbers **925** and **920** respectively before being withdrawn from capital stock in 1910/12. Twenty five years of active service was followed by over fifty inactive ones whilst fulfiling this purpose. They were eventually cut up by a local contractor at Newton Heath shed as late as July 1967, the only locos to be so treated there. Rumour has it that the scrap men got the copper fireboxes out ready to take away the following morning only to discover that they had been stolen overnight!
4th JULY 1963 ● R.S. GREENWOOD

Looking towards Woodlands Road from Queens Road overbridge. A low level splitting signal stands beyond the box whose arms are designated as follows:

Left   Queens Road Up Home - Cheetham Hill Jct.
Below Cheetham Hill Jct Up Outer Distant
Right Queens Road Up Home - Irk Valley
Below Irk Valley Up Outer Distant

Spouting its many chimneys beyond the junction in the background is Kennett House. This fine art deco style building was known locally as 'the ship' or 'Queen Mary', and in its heyday these flats (or modern day apartments) were the height of luxury with all mod cons on site. The concept, however, was considered too advanced for its time and the building was demolished in the early 1970's.

4th JULY 1968 ● ALLAN SOMMERFIELD

QUEENS ROAD GARAGE

Crossley Mancunian No 424 (AND 419) stands in Boyle Street alongside the charming row of houses which fronted on to the side of the bus garage. Unfortunately a few of the residents frequently complained to the Corporation about the persistent noise levels, particularly during unsocial hours!

APRIL 1934 ● A.D. PACKER

An impressive line up of vehicles stand in the washing bays at the rear of Queens Road Garage. *From L-R they are:* No **189** (VR 6008). This was a most significant bus as it was the first of a batch of 19 ordered to directly replace the tramcars which had served the Corporation for nigh on 60 years. The order was placed in September 1929 and they came new to Queens Road Garage from March 1930. These Crossley Lowbridge buses had 'Condor' chassis and 'Piano Front' wooden bodywork and were specifically earmarked for the intensive 53 service, the first to hand over to motor bus operation. The 8 mile journey from Cheetham Hill Road (outside the garage) to Brooks's Bar circled the city, travelling 3/4 of its circumference, crossing many major roads in the process. The rigours of such work affected the timber frames and in December 1934, No 189 received a replacement body of all metal Standard design, as did other members of the batch. Three years later, the body and number transferred to No 346, a later period vehicle which then ran for a further ten years. She was withdrawn in January 1947 and sold to R. Blair, Breaker and Dealer, of Russell Street, Manchester for scrap. Fittingly No 189 carries No 53 and Cheetham Hill Road on her blinds. No **466 (**AVM 151) is another first example of a batch of 35 introduced in 1934. She possessed a Crossley 'Mancunian' chassis with Metro Cammel/Crossley all metal standard bodywork. Sister vehicle No **477** (AVM 331) stands alongside and just in view is No **514** (AXJ 981), a later example of the same type. The washing bays have since become the lower hall within the Manchester Museum of Transport.

APRIL 1934 ● A.D. PACKER

A busy junction was the crossing of Queens Road and Rochdale Road near Queens Park, Collyhurst. Daimler CVG6 No **4189** (KND 950) makes for the city and then onward to Sale Moor, Derbyshire Road South on the 113 service from Moston. This was the last example of a batch of 90 delivered in 1950/1, all of which worked out of Princess Road Garage. A 7' 6" Leyland Titan PD1/1 No **3038** (GVR 240) from Rochdale Road Garage is bound for Moston, Ben Brierley. Standing on the corner is the *Milan Inn* whose distinctive premises were first licensed in 1850 as a beer house. Formerly a tied house of Kays Atlas Brewery, Longsight, it was one of twenty-three purchased by Robinsons Brewery in 1929 with a publican's licence being granted 20 years later. Rather unusually, within the building to the right of the entrance was a UCP snack bar which after the days of steam became a baby shop! Note the Scammell-Scarab in BR livery bringing up the rear, possibly returning to Oldham Road Goods Depot. **25th APRIL 1955 ● RAY DUNNING**

ICI BLACKLEY

0-6-0 side tank 'The Lady Armaghdale' stands in the interchange sidings north of Woodlands Road Halt in Lower Crumpsall at the head of the privately owned ICI mineral railway branch. Built by Hunslet in 1898, this loco was bought by ICI from the Manchester Ship Canal Company on 1st May 1963 to replace saddle tank No 3455 which had been involved in an accident *(see below)*. Her work involved the transfer of 400 tons of coal per day to the dye works to fuel the industrial power stations' boilers. At Trafford Park, the loco carried the name 'St. John' and was numbered 14. After purchase she received a new cherry red livery, her cab windows were enlarged and the original 'Lady Armaghdale' plates were affixed on the tank sides. The loco is happily preserved in working order after being sold to The Warwickshire Industrial Locomotive Preservation Society in December 1968 and operates on the Severn Valley Railway out of Bridgnorth. Woodlands House stands on the hill behind the engine and originally acted as a doctors' residence for nearby Crumpsall Hospital before being utilised by ICI as a social club for executives of the company.

20th JULY 1963 ● C.A. APPLETON

The other loco employed by ICI was 'Isabel'. This Hawthorn Leslie 0-6-0 saddle tank, numbered 3437 and built in 1919, is shunting vans in the heart of the complex - some 3/4 mile from the BR connection at Woodlands Road. *Isabel,* named after the daughter of the founder of the company, Mr Levinstein, also survives in preservation, at the Somerset & Dorset Railway Museum on the West Somerset Railway. ICI Blackley was one of the major research, production and distribution centres within their Dyestuffs Division and the loco is seen surrounded by warehouses containing finished goods. One unfortunate consequence of ICI's activities was that the pigeons nesting in the area tended to assume rather unnatural colours and many ornithological rarities were spotted in the local streets of Blackley and Crumpsall!

10th AUGUST 1953 ● C.A. APPLETON

'The Lady Armaghdale' nameplates were originally carried by this 0-6-0 saddle tank, Hawthorn Leslie No 3455, delivered new in 1920. The laboratories are behind the loco and the slope running away to the right leads towards Delaunay's Road at Crumpsall Vale. 'Lady Armaghdale' was the wife of a former director of the ICI company.

21st MAY 1953 ● B. ROBERTS

WOODLANDS ROAD HALT

Woodlands Road Halt was the first stop out of Manchester Victoria on the 1,200V d.c. Bury electrified line. Opening on 3rd March 1913, facilities here were somewhat primitive and the boarded platforms offered commuters of the Smedley and Lower Crumpsall districts (better known locally as the home of the CWS Biscuit Works) access into the city. Unfortunately the small signalbox here was a target for political extremists and was burnt to the ground during June 1921. The original L&Y stock remained in service for many years and was fondly remembered. The five-car sets of all metal construction were capable of accommodating up to 389 passengers during rush hour periods. They were built locally at the Company's Carriage Works at Newton Heath in 1915 although servicing and repairs were undertaken at Bury where the original East Lancashire Railway workshops (alongside the steam depot) had been converted for the purpose. **1950 ● STATIONS UK**

CRUMPSALL STATION

A tranquil scene looking down Station Road, Crumpsall. The station building was constructed using a distinctive yellow and cream brick whilst the canopy displays L&Y signage proudly advertising 'Trains to Manchester and Bury every few minutes'. Today's residents can enjoy a similar frequency thanks to the introduction of Metrolink, retaining a connection with Bury and the city (and beyond). The office of John Weedall and Co was a landmark on Crumpsall Lane. Their half-timbered premises in the background served traffic relating to the nearby ICI works at Blackley. The road transport is also of interest. A solitary period automobile waits by the station entrance whilst over the road, a steam lorry stands parked beyond the pillar box. Apparently a Bristol A-type bus No 61 (NF 4079) had a slight altercation with the station canopy here whilst working from ICI Blackley on an extra service. **c.1920 ● A. HAYNES COLLECTION**

Crumpsall boasted a busy goods yard offering, in the main, coal facilities for the local merchants. It was situated north of the station on the Up side immediately beyond Crumpsall Lane bridge. Traffic leaving the yard could either gain the Up main line at the throat of the yard or south of the platforms by way of a running loop which passed behind the station buildings. One of Bury Depot's duties was to provide power for the daily pick-up goods which eventually worked through to Brindle Heath Sorting Sidings. After the demise of the Lanky 'A' Class, Austerity 2-8-0's were usually employed, as is the case here with No **90205.** It was not uncommon, however, to find a stranger on the job and, in contrast with the grubby WD, a gleaming loco, ex-Horwich Works running in, occasionally brightened up proceedings. Behind the sidings is the Crumpsall area off Wilton Road beyond which lay the reservoirs adjoining Bowker Bank works. The high rise flats in the distance stand off Blackley New Road.

10th OCTOBER 1963 ● C.A. APPLETON

A cheeky young girl carrying a rather impressive floral arrangement poses for the camera on the Up platform. The morning sun shines kindly on Elsie Haynes before she jumps on to an electric train, due to arrive shortly from the Heaton Park direction, for the 2.5 mile onward journey to Manchester Victoria Station. Later in the day, Elsie, in her Sunday best, will take part in the traditional Whit Walks through the city streets. This annual event brought together hundreds of children from all over the area and was witnessed by many a proud parent.

MAY 1928 ● A. HAYNES COLLECTION

A morning Victoria-bound commuter train enters Crumpsall Station Up platform shortly before withdrawal. The ageing, vestibuled all-metal stock was replaced in 1960 by new Class 504 units of BR design built at Wolverton Works. The interiors of the L&Y stock retained the original seating arrangements with pairs of back-to-back rattan upholstered seats with reversibles placed in between. They were originally painted dark brown below the waist with the remainder light green. The roofs were white although liveries were to change during the later periods. Note the straphangers and somewhat spartan raw light bulbs, one of which is already 'past its sell-by date'. **14th OCTOBER 1959 ● R.S. GREENWOOD**

An evocative view of Crumpsall Green where an unknown photographer has recorded a scene of much interest. To the left, a magnificent gas standard lamp is nicely highlighted as a young girl stares, possibly wondering why a man is standing in the middle of a cobbled Oak Road with camera. The lengthy foreground shadows are cast by Crumpsall Park Methodist Church. The park itself lay to the right, further down the road. The premises of the 'District Bank Limited' had previously been occupied by Crumpsall Green Post Office which, in the days prior to the Grouping, were agents for both the 'Cheshire Lines Railway' and 'Great Northern Railway'. As such they may have been considered to be a distant outpost of the King's Cross empire! A Karrier bus en-route from Cheetham Hill Village to Blackley Village, takes a breather before setting off down Delaunay's Road. The terminus in Blackley was situated below and behind the tram office on Rochdale Road by the Conservative Club. Crumpsall (Crummy) Lane School stands in the background, partially hidden by a tree in full season.   **c.1924** ● **A. HAYNES COLLECTION**

Crescent Road looking towards Lower Crumpsall. The 1924 built Karrier bus has just passed the corner of Oak Road on its way between Cheetham Hill Village and Rochdale Road, Harpurhey. Known as the 'Lower Crumpsall route', both this and the 'Higher Crumpsall' equivalent *(see above)* were the first Manchester northern suburban bus routes and were designed for one man operation. As such they were the forerunners of the type of service we associate with today. This particular class of Karrier bus, however, was not too successful. Lasting only a few years, all six within the class had been disposed of by 1928, although they were among the first vehicles to be fitted with pneumatic tyres. Just out of view down the hill, the road forked forming Springfield Road and Church Road over which spanned a rather impressive viaduct carrying the mineral railway which led to the ICI Blackley complex.   **c.1924** ● **A. HAYNES COLLECTION**

Leyland PD2/40 No 3595 (UNB 595) climbs out of Lower Crumpsall up Harpurhey Road towards Rochdale Road on its way to Brookdale Park. Before the war Queens Road Garage shared the service with Salford Corporation buses working out of Weaste Garage. Certain buses worked beyond the Brookdale Park terminus to Lord Lane, whilst at the other end of the route, some started out from Cheetham Hill Road. The many additional buses serving Crumpsall Hospital ran as 7X's, irrespective of the route they took. The long flight of steps to the former Central Avenue led from the junction of Cypress Street and Ash Street and continued over the road into the vale by the reservoirs and the CWS Biscuit works.

11th JUNE 1967 ● P. J. THOMPSON

Before the war, the Collyhurst branch of Boots Chemists was just one of many thriving shops and businesses in the immediate area flanking the busy thoroughfare of Rochdale Road. By the mid 1950's, in common with the trolleybus, the area was on the wane and within the next decade or so, much of this property would be swept away. A Leyland TB5 4 wheel trolleybus No 1109 (GNA 27) works a No 212 service from Moston Gardener's Arms to Church Street. The pedestrians seem oblivious to its passing by, but this would be the last occasion for them to witness the event - the next day would bring a new motorbus service on to Rochdale Road - Nos 112 and 113! An unidentified pre-war Leyland TD5 on a 7X from Crumpsall Hospital, returning to the city, brings up the rear.

24th APRIL 1955 ● RAY DUNNING

From Moston, Gardener's Arms to Manchester, Stevenson Square, there was much to interest the railway enthusiast travelling on the upper deck of a No 54 bus. After passing the back of Lightbowne Carriage sidings, the route continued down Northampton Road, skirting the former L&Y Carriage Works. Leyland PD2/3 No 3229 (JND 630) is passing the imposing St. Edmunds RC church on Monsall Street, Collyhurst and will shortly cross over the Manchester 'loop line' at the junction of Gateforth Street. From here it will pass down Queens Road, offering glimpses of Tank Yard and Brewery Sidings before passing under Miles Platting junction. A right hand turn at the Playhouse corner took the bus on to Oldham Road which runs parallel with the original Manchester and Leeds Railway and into the city. Two days after the photograph, Service 54 was replaced by an extension of Service 80 from the Gardener's Arms to Middleton. 19th MARCH 1966 ● P. J. THOMPSON

Trains heading up the Calder Valley Main Line out of Manchester Victoria Station faced a continual climb to Rochdale. The maximum gradient of 1 in 63 is on this section between Smedley Viaduct and Thorpes Bridge Junction. Jubilee 4-6-0 No **45698 *Mars*** storms past Monsall Lane signalbox with a Newcastle relief train. The loco is always associated as being one of the trio at Bank Hall but this was not always the case. She spent her early years at Newton Heath before taking up residence on Merseyside on 12th October 1946. During her lifetime the loco was attached to a number of tenders. Introduced into service in 1936, she was initially paired with a Fowler 3,500 gallon example but during the 1940-48 period she had the larger, Stanier 4,000 gallon type for company. Before Nationalisation, the Operating Department decided that the Fowler Un-rebuilt Royal Scots would take preference in the handling of many of the principal express workings and they received the larger Stanier tenders from the Jubilees in exchange. No 45698 has recently been re-attached to one of these Fowler tenders which, incidentally, carries no crest yet is fully lined out, unlike the engine. On 29th April 1959 she was finally re-acquainted with a Stanier tender, this time off an 8F 2-8-0 loco which remained with her until withdrawal in November 1965. c.1950 ● **ARTHUR BENDELL**

L&Y 4-4-0 No 1112 passes the box on the Down Slow line. Note the signal gantry which was removed in early 1912 at the time when Newton Heath (Monsall Lane) Carriage Sidings went out of commission. The arms controlling the Down Fast and Down Fast to Down Slow appear over the leading carriage. The lower quadrant Down Home Slow is off (over the second carriage) whilst the soon to be redundant signal, that above the rear of the train, controls the reception line leading to the extensive carriage sidings. (*Compare with the photograph above which shows the simplified arrangement*). In 1909 the approximate stabling capacity at Monsall Lane was 184 coaches and was of similar size to nearby Red Bank and Lightbowne. The other local carriage sidings serving Victoria were Queens Road (94), Cheetham Hill (66), Newtown (67) and Irlam (60). c.1910 ● **J. E. KITE**

THORPES BRIDGE JUNCTION

This low angle view focuses in the foreground on perhaps one of the most traversed sections of track within the BR network - the main access road to Newton Heath MPD. Thorpes Bridge Junction Signalbox, standing behind the 25mph speed restriction sign, controlled most movements on and off the shed as well as those in the immediate area. The exception to this were the Up and Down fast lines on the 'Manchester Loop' which fall away to the right, under the bridge - this section came under the control of Monsall Lane and Newton Heath Junction boxes. Straight ahead in the distance beyond the signal gantry were the extensive Brewery Sidings, situated on the Down side of the line towards Miles Platting, opposite which were the premises of Matthew Swain.

MARCH 1968 ● TED PARKER

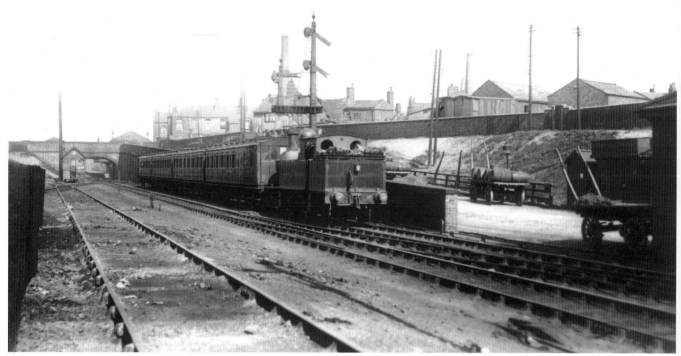

One of Aspinall's most famous classes was the ubiquitous L&Y 2-4-2 tank. No **18** was the first in the final series of 20 locos built in 1911 with Schmidt superheaters and Belpaire fireboxes. They were given express engine rank from the outset and shared the top diagrams with the more illustrious 'Highflyers' and 'Dreadnoughts'. Whilst working one such duty, sister loco No 276 derailed at speed with fatal consequences. The Inspecting Officer deemed that, despite the class's undoubted power and efficiency, they were to be relegated to lesser duties. By 1913 all 20 engines were concentrated at Newton Heath for work on the Oldham, Rochdale and other local services. Having left Dean Lane Station, No 18 is nearing Thorpes Bridge Junction with a train from Oldham made up of Attock stock. The signal is of interest - the old style arm being crowned by a wooden ball finial and controlled by Dean Lane and Engine Shed No 1 signalbox in the distance. This was constructed in 1880, four years after the opening of the engine shed. Access on and off the depot could also be gained via Thorpes Bridge and Newton Heath Junction signalboxes. Dean Lane box, constructed by the Gloucester Wagon Company, closed on 28th July 1957. **1914 ● REAL PHOTOS**

An unidentified Stanier Class Five offers assistance to a train of vans destined for Oldham Clegg Street depot. The working of freight traffic to the Oldham district was diverted via Dean Lane, Failsworth and Hollinwood - a line which had previously seen little activity of this nature. A banking loco (nearly always a Class Five by this time) was stationed at Thorpes Bridge junction to assist trains which were faced with gradients of up to 1 in 50 for over more than three miles.

MARCH 1968 ● TED PARKER

Newton Heath Motive Power Depot had the distinction of receiving the first red liveried Hughes/Fowler 'Crab' 2-6-0 into service. A total of 245 were built at Horwich and Crewe between 1926 and 1932 but were renumbered 2700-2944 from 1934. The prototype, No **13000** stands on the spur between Dean Lane Signalbox and the overbridge but is no longer in ex-works condition. These engines soon became popular with locomen and covered a wide range of duties over the ex-L&Y system.

1926 ● JOHN RYAN COLLECTION

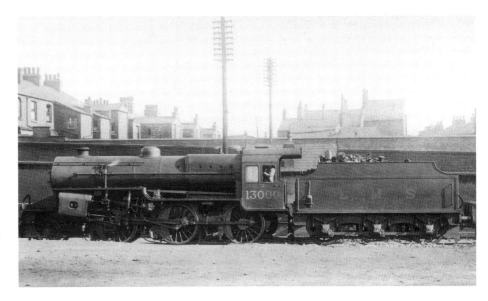

DEAN LANE STATION

Coal for Higginshaw Gas Works had to traverse the steeply graded Thorpes Bridge Junction to Oldham line after the embargo on freight via the much easier route through Milnrow. Stanier Class Five 4-6-0 No **44884** (12A), fitted with bufferbeam snowplough, makes an all out assault through Dean Lane Station. A brake van is at each end of a lengthy rake of fully loaded Standard BR 16 ton mineral wagons. The snowplough is a legacy from the days when Carlisle Kingmoor came under the control of the Scottish Region (prior to mid-1958), during which time the shed code was 68A.

SEPTEMBER 1967 ● PAUL JORDAN

The going away shot shows the train with an unidentified Stanier 8F 2-8-0 bringing up the rear, offering much needed assistance. Also recording the scene further along the Dean Lane Up platform platform are photographers Jeff Clough and Eric Humphrey (who has one of the ubiquitous duffle bags over his shoulder). The neglect of the station and its environs are all too evident with overgrown platforms and derelict gas lamps. A shadow board gave the driver a better view of the starting signal immediately in front of Reliance Street bridge, this being controlled from Thorpes Bridge Junction Signalbox.

SEPTEMBER 1967 ● PAUL JORDAN

The official entrance to Newton Heath Depot was gained from Dean Lane at a point almost opposite the station entrance. Nearby ran the A62, the major trunk road to Oldham and beyond into Yorkshire. Numerous buses plied this road but only two routes actually operated down Dean Lane. One was service No 7 which ran between Mandley Park and Brookdale Park. This curious route was a Queens Road Garage duty who provided Leyland Titan PD2/3's for many years. One such vehicle is No **3223** (JND 624) seen passing the station. The destination blind indicates the bus has travelled by way of Crumpsall, Harpurhey and Moston. The other was service No 65, which crossed the city from Trafford Park to Moston, Gardener's Arms by way of Piccadilly, the A62 and New Moston. Princess Road and Hyde Road Garages shared this route so one was more likely to see buses of Crossley and Daimler origin at work. After Rochdale Road became 'bus only' in 1955, the garage took over Hyde Road's duties on the No 65. The upper decks afforded splendid views of the east yard and St Mary's Road turntable. Of further interest is the Bedford Duple coach in the background which may be transporting trainspotters as members of a railway society. Next stop Gorton Shed and Works?

1962 ● R.H.G. SIMPSON

Hollinwood tram terminus was situated on the original Failsworth and Oldham Borough boundary. Looking in the Manchester direction, a pair of Oldham Corporation cars are about to depart in opposite directions. That nearest the camera is No **16**, working service No 8 from here to Shaw, Wren's Nest via Werneth and Featherstall Road. The other car, No **12**, has paused whilst working the jointly operated through No 20 service between Waterhead and Manchester, Stevenson Square. The Shaw route closed just after the outbreak of war, leaving only the No 20. The end of the Oldham trams came on 3rd August 1946, an occasion recognised by officialdom as a decorated balcony car ran proudly through the streets sporting signs 'honourably retiring'.

1937 ● W.A. CAMWELL

HOLLINWOOD

The four track terminus looking north towards Oldham. Manchester Car No **979** is about to return working on the part day service No 21 which extended to Piccadilly. The Oldham Car in the rear is No **24**, again waiting on the No 8 to Shaw, Wren's Nest. The motorbus standing by the boundary sign is Oldham Corporation No **19** (BU 8255), one of only three 1934 Leyland TS6's with full fronted Roe body, dedicated to route No 13 - Manchester, Parker Street to Uppermill via Scouthead. The service was introduced on 4th December 1932 and was jointly operated by Manchester, Oldham and North Western Road Car Co Ltd. **1937** ● **W.A. CAMWELL**

Newton Heath Shed was by far the largest of the 32 depots established within the former L&Y system. It was coded '1' from the outset in 1876 and constituted its own district for many years. A depot of such magnitude cannot be adequately covered within the scope of this work and will be the subject of a further volume in due course. These three views, all taken in the west yard on the reception road near to the coaling plant, overlook the Calder Valley main line and Lightbowne Carriage sidings.

TOP: **Hughes** 'Dreadnought' 4-6-0 No **10446** (C1).
JUNE 1937 ● GORDON COLTAS

MIDDLE: **Aspinall** rebuild of Barton Wright Class 23 0-6-0 to 0-6-0 Saddle Tank No **51343** (26A).
9th NOVEMBER 1957 ● JIM PEDEN

BOTTOM: **Stanier** rebuild of Fowler 4-6-0 'Royal Scot' loco. No **46163** *Civil Service Rifleman* (5A).
24th AUGUST 1955 ● BRIAN MORRISON

LIGHTBOWNE CARRIAGE SIDINGS

A stranger in the camp! Perhaps one of the most unusual observations in and around Lightbowne (or Newton Heath MPD for that matter), was this J39 0-6-0 No **64903** hailing from Low Moor (Bradford) depot. Thankfully recorded for posterity from a passing train, it seems even more remarkable considering that the usual hive of activity on the opposite side of the line at this point, ie the busy shed yard, would normally attract the enthusiast's attention. After running in, the ex-LNER loco, in ex-works condition, is working home following a lengthy visit to nearby Gorton Works for heavy inter-mediate repair (28th July - 30th September).

17th OCTOBER 1959 ● R. S. GREENWOOD

The Lightbowne Pilot duty was in the hands of a 'Breadvan' for many years, after which a variety of classes were to be seen performing the task. Ivatt Class 2 2-6-0 No **46504** is caught resting between empty coaching stock duties. This was the second example of a final batch of 25 of these versatile locos built at Swindon Works in 1952/3 (Lot 394). They were earmarked for the Western Region and many were delivered new to Oswestry shed. Following a spell at Bolton, this loco gravitated to Newton Heath for its final two months in service before being withdrawn in October 1966. Beneath the layers of grime, one could just about detect the 'Swindon green' livery carried in later years.

SEPTEMBER 1966 ● PAUL JORDAN

A spot of bother sees Hughes/Fowler 'Crab' 2-6-0 No **42707's** tender off the rails. Carrying the short lived British Railways lettering, it would appear that the rear axle may be the cause of the derailment. Incidents such as this were commonplace at Lightbowne where the condition of the permanent way left much to be desired. Meanwhile a group of men, including the crew, contemplate the situation. The engine remained at Newton Heath throughout the fifties before moving on to Fleetwood (24F) in January 1960. Later that year, (Tuesday, 28th June), No 42707 was one of a number of locos stabled within Preston Shed, the building of which was destroyed by a fire which caught hold of the wooden roof. Unlike others, the 'Crab' survived and remained in service for a further three years. **1951 ● ARTHUR BENDELL**

Stalwart Jubilee 4-6-0 No 45698 *Mars* makes a fine sight passing between the Carriage Shed and Newton Heath depot. The train may well be a relief to the morning Newcastle as it is loaded to 11 bogies rather than the usual smart set of 9 carmine and cream liveried examples. The extra load has necessitated banking assistance from Victoria and the engine can just be seen 'dropping off' at this point. *Mars* lost her Fowler tender in April 1959 in favour of a Stanier example - much to the relief of the Bank Hall enginemen.   **AUGUST 1953** ● **ARTHUR BENDELL**

Still carrying her reporting number C530, Stanier Class 8F 2-8-0 No **48455** is unusually employed bringing a train of non-corridor empty stock under Thorpes Bridge. The loco hails from Birkenhead (6C) shed and the coaches will shortly set back to be stabled in Lightbowne Carriage Sidings.   **12th APRIL 1957** ● **H.C. CASSERLEY**

When Manchester United entertained Preston North End in a Northern League fixture during the 1945-46 season, Accrington provided Lostock Hall men with ex-L&Y 'A' Class 0-6-0 No **12101** to bring their supporters into town. They detrained at Manchester Victoria after which the loco brought the stock up to Lightbowne Sidings for stabling. She then spent a couple of hours on shed before picking it up again for the return journey. The fireman is setting about breaking up large chunks of replenished coal with the pick whilst awaiting the signal 'off shed' from Newton Heath Junction box. Departure time was 6.00pm, giving fans ample time to reach Victoria. The game was played at Maine Road because of war damage inflicted at Old Trafford, but it would be a sombre return journey - Preston were thrashed 6-1.

3rd NOVEMBER 1945 ● W. COOPER

Driver Robinson of Newton Heath shed, rarely seen without a cigarette hanging from his lower lip, casts a backward glance from the footplate of his LMS 0-8-0 'Austin Seven' No **9643**. He has clear signals from the Junction box to transfer from Down Slow to Fast with a train of mineral empties before heading up the Calder Valley. This was one of many such workings which started out from the nearby Brewery Sidings and was destined for Healey Mills. A dirty fire does nothing but further pollute the atmosphere here and with signs of steam escaping from the inside cylinders, the driver may report the loco for examination on arrival at Wakefield depot.

3rd NOVEMBER 1945 ● W. COOPER

A visitor from Mirfield sidles around the side of the shed before being stabled in the East yard. Austerity 2-8-0 No **90655** was one of a handful of the class which still operated from this depot although examples from Normanton and Wakefield depots also made regular visits.

1966 ● PAUL JORDAN

RIGHT **A Bolton Class Five** makes a stirring sight passing the east end of the shed at 6.50pm in the evening with a coal train. No **45377** was one of many Stanier and Standard 4-6-0's based at the depot by this time although when No 45290 arrived in February 1962, it was the largest engine the ex-L&Y depot had ever received on its allocation.

25th MAY 1967 ● ERIC HUMPHREY

NEWTON HEATH JUNCTION

A fine panoramic view from the footbridge looking towards Manchester. The loco depot and yard occupy the left background behind the splitting signals whilst the magnitude of Lightbowne Sidings and their environs can be appreciated here. A portion of the former L&Y Carriage and Wagon Works complex shows two buildings, each containing sixteen roads on the Lightbowne side of Thorp Road. Further carriage sidings, which largely held excursion stock, extended towards Lightbowne Road and are out of view to the right of the photograph! It is hard to imagine that Dean Lane originally passed under the station at this point. The original bridge abutment behind the building on the Down platform offers a clue. The lane was truncated behind the Railway Hotel in the early 1930's allowing the LMS to develop the East yard of the depot as part of the 1935 modernisation scheme.
c.1956 ● T. A. FLETCHER

Hard at work one icy winter's morning is LMS-built Ivatt Class 2 2-6-0 No **46417**, looking worse for wear and seen here shortly before withdrawal, reversing alongside the shed buildings to pick up wagons of loco coal. The history of this loco is of interest. She was one of a second batch of ten within the building programme of Ivatt. Lot 189 - Crewe Order E465 - saw Nos 6410-19 enter service on 1st March 1947. The loco spent her entire life on the Central Division, initially being one of four (Nos 6414-17) going new to Bank Hall. She then became a long standing resident of Bury (26D), having moved on there in January 1955, but the closure of the Buckley Wells Depot on 12th April 1965 prompted a move 'down the road' to Bolton. The stay here was short lived and in August 1966 she arrived, fittingly, at the Central Lines' principal depot to work out her final six months in service.

JANUARY 1967 ● PAUL JORDAN

Pottering about behind the station is Johnson Midland Class 3F 0-6-0T No **47207**. Introduced in 1899 and rebuilt with a Belpaire firebox in 1919, she was one of a class which numbered 60 locos, many of which were based at Cricklewood. They were fitted with condensing apparatus for working over the Metropolitan Widened Lines with cross-London freights to and from the Southern Region. The signalmen working at Newton Heath Junction box were in a fine position to observe, but not control, the almost continuous activity at times between the loco coal sidings, situated behind Newton Heath station, and the coaling plant.

JANUARY 1963 ● KEN NUTTALL

The Coal Stage Pilot duty in the hands of ex-L&Y No **52159**.

**9th NOVEMBER 1957 ●
JIM PEDEN**

The 26A shedplate fitted to Stanier 8F 2-8-0 No 48718 was short lived. It arrived from Northwich in October 1950 but it had departed for pastures new (Birkenhead) by the following year. This was part of a major motive power reorganisation which brought large numbers of ex-WD 2-8-0s on to the Central Division in exchange for Stanier's version. No 48718 brings a lengthy mixed freight from the Miles Platting direction on to the Calder Valley main line at Newton Heath Junction. The east end of the shed appears unusually quiet and smoke free. Two footplatemen await the passage of the train before crossing to gain access to either Newton Heath Station's Down platform or Lightbowne Carriage Sidings.   **1950 ● ARTHUR BENDELL**

The 5.37pm Fridays Only Manchester Exchange - York was one of the last regular steam hauled passenger services to traverse the Calder Valley route. As a consequence it became a magnet for enthusiasts wishing to record the passage of a train rostered for a Carlisle Kingmoor locomotive. The working usually produced a Britannia Pacific but on this occasion, Stanier Class Five No **44767** makes good progress approaching the now derelict Newton Heath Station. This loco happily survives in preservation.   **14th JULY 1967 ● PAUL JORDAN**

On weekdays during 1963, two trains departed for Southport from Victoria within ten minutes of each other. The first, departing from Platform 15 at 4.00pm was all stations, arriving at Chapel Street at 5.34pm. The second, from Platform 11 was express, calling at Wigan (Wallgate) only and arriving on the coast 34 minutes earlier. Standard Class 4 4-6-0 No **75048** has just coupled up to the empty stock behind Newton Heath Junction signalbox, which will form the stopping service. **18th SEPTEMBER 1963 ● PAUL JORDAN**

One of Patricroft's large stud of Caprotti Standard Class 5's, No 73133 drifts towards the reception road at the depot having worked light engine from Castleton. 30 out of a class of 172 locos had British Caprotti valves and gear of the latest design - they were mechanically efficient machines and were easily maintained. The makeshift front numberplate and general condition of the loco was all too common a sight towards the end of steam. Original number and shedplates, together with worksplates, were beginning to attract a market value.

18th SEPTEMBER 1967 ● PAUL SHACKCLOTH

A locomotive regularly entrusted to working the 4.37pm Manchester Victoria - Halifax train was Standard Class 4MT 4-6-0 No **75018,** as part of a more extensive Southport diagram. On this occasion, however, she is captured ambling sedately through Newton Heath Junction with a train of non-corridor empty stock - an unusual working as this was Boxing Day! Amongst the visitors spending Christmas on shed were ex-Midland 4F 0-6-0 No 43932, recently transferred from Saltley to Gorton, and WD 2-8-0 No 90013 from Frodingham.

26th DECEMBER 1961 ● DON CASH

NEWTON HEATH STATION

Carnforth Class Five No 44709 passes through the weed infested platforms with a Manchester Victoria to Blackpool North parcels train via Bury Knowsley Street. After the station's closure it became a safe haven for local trainspotters. No longer did they have to endure the wrath of 'Nasty Ned', a station porter who took an instant dislike to enthusiasts encroaching on his patch. Jeff Clough was one who spent many happy hours there. He had positioned himself on the footbridge to record the train whilst his mates, Eric Humphrey, Paul Jordan and Bernard Crick sought out other photographic vantage points. The boy on the platform wasn't in the gang though. A two-car Cravens DMU takes the Up Slow line towards the city, beyond which is a rake of mineral wagons awaiting their turn to individually dispense the contents of loco coal into the hopper. A great number of coaches are still to be found in the depths of Lightbowne Sidings as well as a grounded body behind the station building.

MARCH 1967 ● JEFF CLOUGH

A poster displayed on the platform spelt out the end. By this time passengers using the facilities here were few and far between and little inconvenience was caused anyway because of the close proximity of Dean Lane Station. Middleton Junction was a different matter though. Note the enamel totem still in situ at the eleventh hour - a desirable item of railwayana in today's market. The station opened for business on 11th July 1846 and remained gas lit throughout. A welcoming coal fire could always be found on both Up and Down platforms in the winter months.

**26th NOVEMBER 1965 ●
RICHARD CORT**

An unusual duty for WD 2-8-0 No 90266. The locomotive is about to depart from Lightbowne Carriage Sidings with a 20 coach empty stock train to Blackpool. The procession will travel by way of Castleton South Junction, Bury Knowsley Street and then via Bolton and Preston. The Austerity had travelled light engine from its home depot at Lostock Hall earlier in the morning to pick up its train. Workings of this sort often took place on Sundays where a path could be more easily be found.

19th AUGUST 1962 ● PAUL JORDAN

EMPTY STOCK -
LIGHTBOWNE CARRIAGE SIDINGS

Stanier Class Five 4-6-0 No 45133 (8B - Warrington Dallam) is about to start out with its stock towards Manchester Victoria Station. The crumbling remains of the station buildings on Newton Heath's Down platform are evident. Even after closure, the station served as a wages point for the local station and signalbox staff. Immediately left of the smokebox door is 'The Alexian Brothers' Nursing Home' on St. Mary's Road, an institution of historical significance. 15th JULY 1967 ● PAUL JORDAN

About to set its stock back into the carriage sidings is unre-built Patriot Class 6P/5F 4-6-0 No **45509 The Derbyshire Yeomanry.** The distinctive coach numbered E86126E is pure Gresley vintage.

11th MARCH 1959 ●
R.S. GREENWOOD

The stopping trains from the Yorkshire town of Normanton to Manchester were largely in the hands of ex-L&Y 2-4-2T's for many years but in BR days an interesting variety of motive power could be seen. LMS 0-6-0 No **44336** from Normanton shed, moves the 11.45 ex-Normanton away from its penultimate stop coupled to a rake of early Midland close-coupled stock. **4th MAY 1952 ● B.K.B. GREEN**

An everyday sight on the Calder Valley main line for almost twenty years were great numbers of WD 2-8-0's handling a constant procession of mineral traffic. Nearly 200 of these locos were based on the ex-L&Y system from 1943 with many working out of Wakefield and Newton Heath depots. On a late Monday afternoon, a typically grubby loco, whose number was barely discernable, rumbles on through, signalled for the Up fast via Cheetham Hill and thereby avoiding the Miles Platting area. A full boiler was necessary for the descent through Manchester Victoria and the fireman is keeping a watchful eye on his injector which is forever dribbling hot water over the sleeper ends.

12th APRIL 1965 ● BERNARD CRICK

Signalled into the running loop north of Newton Heath Station is 'Austin Seven' 0-8-0 No **49508,** destined to be the last member of its class. The main line was regained immediately south of Colliery Junction after having passed through its own set of arches over the unusual St. Mary's Road bridge. Such was the concentration of traffic over the Calder Valley line, it was not unusual for an empty mineral train travelling in the Healey Mills direction taking all day from the Manchester area, resulting in enginemen having to lodge at Wakefield shed. Similarly the 64-bed Newton Heath barracks catered for those based at Yorkshire depots, having been held in passing loops in the Up direction. No 49508 was based at Bury at the time and in all probability is working in that direction, leaving the main line at Castleton South Junction with its mixed freight.

15th APRIL 1951 ● ARTHUR BENDELL

The 5.10pm Victoria to York hurries through Newton Heath station in the hands of the usual Thompson B1 4-6-0 loco. York (Clifton) Depot had plenty of this type to call on for this duty (the allocation numbered thirteen on 1st January 1952) and only rarely did they have to either 'borrow' one or use another class. Gresley V2 2-6-2's would have been the ideal substitute but they were officially prohibited on the LM section of the Calder Valley line. One of 50A's regulars, No **61053** leaves a haze of smoke over Lightbowne on her way to Rochdale.

JUNE 1952 ● **ARTHUR BENDELL**

The Heaton - Red Bank empty newspaper train produced many interesting combinations over the years. The train, usually loaded to over 20 vans, traversed the Calder Valley main line and became something of a high profile working amongst local enthusiasts. Carlisle's Britannia Pacifics became a regular sight in the latter years after having worked the 5.37pm Manchester Exchange to York via the same route the previous evening. One such loco, Upperby's No **70018 Flying Dutchman** is piloting ex-LNER B1 4-6-0 No **61030 Nyala** from Wakefield shed, both bereft of nameplates. The photograph is taken from the footbridge spanning Newton Heath's station platforms, which also offered an excellent view of the east yard. A variety of locos stand stabled on the remaining shed roads, with the diesel maintenance depot also prominent. The train was notorious for late running but on this occasion the recorded passing time of 5.50pm meant it was on schedule.

28th MAY 1966 ● **PAUL JORDAN COLLECTION**

A locomotive allocated to Newton Heath for some considerable time was Hughes 'Crab' 2-6-0 No **42709**. These sturdy engines were often engaged on excursion traffic and were a common sight on the Calder Valley main line. Engine and non-corridor stock clatter over St. Mary's Road Bridge, known locally as the 'hoop' bridge. Loco and train are about to pass through Newton Heath station in this view looking north.

c.1959 ● J. DAVENPORT

ST. MARY'S ROAD

The driver of Standard 9F 2-10-0 No **92004** proceeds with caution through the station, over Newton Heath Junction and on to shed with his loco. The triangle of land now occupied by the Shell garage behind the perimeter fence was once a haven for trainspotters, the majority of whom enjoyed a football 'kickabout' during those quieter periods. The hole in the platform fencing offered an unofficial way of getting into the shed. The first number in the book would be withdrawn Ivatt Class 2 2-6-0 No **46412**.

NOVEMBER 1966 ● PAUL JORDAN

The notorious headshunt at Lightbowne Sidings can be clearly seen in this panoramic view. More than one runaway had been reported over the years but perhaps the most serious incident concerned a Lanky 'A' class, whose braking power was insufficient for its train of empty stock down the falling gradient. Apparently the loco nearly ended up in the back yard of a house on St Mary's Road! Beyond the headshunt a Standard Class Five slogs eastbound with a mineral train. The Newton Heath area is one of great geological interest. The deep ravine in the foreground was cut by Moston Brook which rose as a spring near Failsworth Station. The Dean Brook joined forces in the ravine (a pub of the same name still stands in the shadow of St Mary's Road 'hoop' bridge) and after flowing through Moston Bottoms, the waters eventually join the River Irk as a tributary directly under Smedley Viaduct Signalbox.

1967 ● JEFF CLOUGH

LIGHTBOWNE ROAD

During the 1950's, the No 54 service was largely in the hands of Leyland PD1/3's working out of Queens Road - but only those examples whose fleet numbers ended with an odd number. The services working along the Rochdale and Oldham Roads had one set of indicator blinds, whilst vehicles working along Cheetham Hill Road had another. Regular observation from Broadhurst Café, at the junction of Lightbowne and Nuthurst Roads where the No 7 and 54 services crossed, revealed that Nos 3101/3/5/7/9/11 and 13 were the buses regularly employed on the 54 route from Middleton to Stevenson Square at 20 minute intervals. Similarly Nos 3102/4/6/8/10 and 12 always seemed to be on the No 7 Mandley Park (Bristol Street) to Newton Heath (Brookdale Park). No **3103** (JNA 404) continues down Lightbowne Road, passing the junction with Kenyon Lane (late Dean Lane). The oval sign bracketed on to the lamp post was made of vitreous enamel and had a red background indicating 'Bus Stage' - ordinary 'Bus Stops' were yellow. These anonymous 'out of town' signs tended to be seen on roads where only a single service would pass, the Corporation perhaps assuming that the locals knew the timetable. MCTD provided a litter bin but no shelter in this case.

7th OCTOBER 1954 ● RAY DUNNING

When Rochdale Road bus drivers took over the workings of the No 211 service, they had already phased themselves in, working alongside the trolleybuses whilst familiarising themselves with the route. These joint operations took place at weekends when the roads tended to be quieter. Leyland PD1/1 No **3041** (GVR 243) saunters down Lightbowne Road on a sunny Saturday afternoon with not another vehicle in sight. Motorbuses, however, had occasionally appeared for a different reason. Towards the end of trolleybus operation, the Moston area suffered a series of electrical breakdowns, resulting in a motley collection of buses arriving from both Queens Road and Hyde Road Garages at short notice. Rochdale Road barely had the extra capacity to cover such unforeseen events.

18th JUNE 1955 ● RAY DUNNING

Leyland TB4 No 1028 (DXJ 979) swings off Lightbowne Road and on to Thorp Road on service No 211 from Moston Gardener's Arms to Stevenson Square. The road climbs sharply from here with the ex-L&Y Carriage Works to the right and Lightbowne and Newton Heath Carriage sidings on the left. After passing over Thorpes Bridge, the trolleybus then reaches the T Junction with Oldham Road by the Ceylon Cinema. Note the excursion stock stabled in the recesses of Lightbowne Sidings and the wall of the adjacent carriage shed. External advertising on Manchester Corporation vehicles appeared from 1950, representing an additional source of revenue. No 1028 was the first member of a second series of 10 vehicles introduced in 1938. She was withdrawn from service in November 1955 with the 211 service having switched to bus operation on 7th August earlier that year.

30th MARCH 1955 ● RAY DUNNING

An unidentified Leyland TB5 trolleybus (1100-36 series) swings off Lightbowne Road on to Kenyon Lane towards the Ben Brierley. On the corner, in the foreground, is a police pillar, a cast iron structure with telephone box and light on top. An inspector is in attendance. By 1928, Manchester had a police telephone system operating from both pillars and boxes, the earliest of which was sited at the nearby Ben Brierley. An emergency public facility was also available. They remained in place within the communications network until well into the 1960's and local officers regularly booked on and off duty by telephone to Divisional Headquarters. Coincidentally, the advent of the Panda Car system coincided with the end of steam in 1968.

7th OCTOBER 1954 ● RAY DUNNING

The Ben Brierley generally referred to as the 'Ben', was named after the Failsworth dialect poet and playwright. Leyland PD1/1 No **3044** (GVR 246) makes a fine sight standing on Moston Lane ready to leave for the last leg of its journey to the Gardener's Arms on the 113 service. Manchester Corporation buses carried external adverts from 1950 onwards and many early examples appear to be brewery related!

18th JUNE 1955 ● R. MACK

THE BEN BRIERLEY

Standing at the terminus alongside the imposing St. Dunstans R.C. Church is Crossley 4 wheel trolleybus No **1013** (DXJ 964). The congregation, meanwhile, spill out of a morning 'Mass' service whilst in the background, on the corner of Worsley Avenue, the 'Teas & Hovis' hanging sign for Martins Café can be seen. Founded in 1922 as a Swiss confectionery bakery - continental fayre was unusual in those days - the business happily survived the closing years of steam.

18th JUNE 1952 ● R. MACK

MOSTON EXCHANGE SIDINGS

A daily working to the sidings involved a Patricroft loco, usually one of their ex-LNWR 'Super D's. She would arrive mid-morning light engine and van before departing almost immediately with wagons transferring goods to Ordsall Lane on the west side of the city. No **49134** is pictured performing the diagram.

6th MARCH 1962 ● PAUL JORDAN

Moston Exchange Sidings lay on the Up side of the main line between Moston and Newton Heath Station. They handled a great throughput of traffic arriving from the North and the activities in and around the yard involved many locos and men. One high profile working was the Moston - Camden Class C freight which brought a Willesden loco into town. The sidings were flanked by the Failsworth Golf Club to the east whose course extended beyond the arrival lines. One of the holes here was reputedly the longest in the Manchester area. Originally the Moston Colliery site and then the subsequent development of the housing estate (known locally as the miner's estate) in view occupied land to the west. On a cold winters day, an unidentified Stanier 8F 2-8-0, badly leaking steam, struggles to maintain progress with freight from Brewery Sidings and has reached the north eastern entrance immediately south of Nuthurst Road bridge.

6th JANUARY 1966 ● PAUL JORDAN

OVERLEAF, TOP: **Engineering work in the area** has resulted in Jubilee 4-6-0 No **45719** *Glorious* working 'wrong line' as far as Colliery Junction box. In addition to the driver being issued with a 'Wrong Line Order Form D' from the signalman, he would be subject to a severe speed restriction. The train is crossing back on to the Down and is about to get back into its stride, no doubt having to make up for lost time. Partially responsible for controlling this movement is Moston Colliery Junction signalbox, seen in the distance. Built by Saxby and Farmer in 1872, this 24-lever box closed on 5th April 1964, some fourteen years after the colliery itself! The signal protecting the incline is visible through the smoke haze. This particular 'Jub' was once on Newton Heath's allocation and, being unpopular with the men was nicknamed 'Gormless'.
1953 ● ARTHUR BENDELL

BOTTOM: **The overgrown embankment** between the main line and the long abandoned colliery branch offers this vantage point overlooking the departure sidings within Moston Exchange Sidings giving plenty of activity. Semaphore signals survive but the splitting distants on the Up line are no more. The small concrete structure immediately left of the loco was provided for the fog signalman after demolition of the nearby box. Stanier Class Five 4-6-0 No **45203** with an extraordinary stockpile of coal in its tender, works a Brewery Sidings to Royton Junction mixed freight. St Mary's Road School is visible over the loco and was opened as a Wesleyan Day School on 5th July 1867. **1967 ● JEFF CLOUGH**

MOSTON COLLIERY JUNCTION

Built in 1913, Hudswell Clark 0-4-0ST No 1036 *Westwood* was the last loco in regular service before the pit closed in 1950. They were housed in their own shed situated at the northern end of the site, adjacent to the old abandoned No 1 shaft, seen in the background. The driver nonchalantly draws on his pipe whilst a rather exposed cab allows a pair of workers, possibly yard men riding on the footplate, to pose for the camera.

1948 ● F. CONSTERDINE

Deep shaft coal mining came to Moston the year following the completion of the Manchester and Leeds Railway through the township in 1839. The first shaft to be sunk was at a point almost adjacent to the line near Nuthurst Road Bridge and, although offering rich potential, it was also susceptible to flooding and was eventually abandoned in 1884. Three other shafts were developed over the years, by which time the firm of Platt Bros and Co Ltd of Oldham, in conjunction with two other local companies, acquired the lease in 1874. Despite years of under-investment, Moston was always considered to be an extremely productive site. In its heyday, immediately prior to World War Two, over 175,000 tons of coal was wound including that of the highest quality - 'Moston Black' - which was extracted from the 'Roger' Mine. The year of 1947 saw the nationalisation of all coal mines which, ironically, came at a time when Platt Bros had decided to invest in the pit by upgrading facilities. These improvements were immediately suspended. Having conducted a review, the National Coal Board decreed the pits' closure amidst scenes of great controversy. Despite having the better development potential, future investment would be at nearby Bradford. Moston Colliery closed on 5th June 1950 although it continued to serve as a ventilation station until Bradford Colliery's eventual demise in 1968. Various industrial locos served here over the years, including: Hawthorn Leslie 0-4-0ST named *Shaw*, Hawthorn Leslie 0-6-0ST named *Failsworth* and Hudswell Clark 0-4-0ST No 1036 *Westwood*. Additionally, other locos owned by Platt Bros appeared from time to time as the situation arose. Access from the main line was by way of a severe incline immediately north of St. Mary's Road bridge off the Down running loop. The nearby Moston Mill was rail connected within the complex and one of the loco's duties was to transport wagons of coal there, crossing Nuthurst Road (or Coal Pit Road as it was formerly known) on the level.

The fireman of ex-LMS 2P 4-4-0 No 40585 stands proud on his footplate, Having been held at the signal for some time, he was fully aware of the photographers presence on the footsteps of Moston Colliery Junction signalbox. The colliery incline lay immediately behind the embankment, access to which was protected by a gate. A note in the 'Central Lines Sectional Appendix' outlined the correct procedure.

c.1949 ● ARTHUR BENDELL

Old favourite - Jubilee 4-6-0 No 45698 *Mars* bursts from under Nuthurst Road bridge with the morning 'Newcastle' restaurant car express. This was a favourite location overlooking the small Moston Junction signalbox for three young trainspotting friends in the late 1950's and early 60's, namely Joe Leighton, Martin Huk and the author. During this period, the 'twenty to twelve', as we knew it, had been cut back to York and the restaurant car dispensed with. This coincided with the introduction of the 'Trans-Pennine' service, routed via Huddersfield, in January 1961. Highlight of the day was undoubtedly the 'double-header' - the very long Heaton - Red Bank empty newspaper train which invariably produced a 'cop'. It was due through between 5 and 5.30pm and on many occasions it would infuriatingly cross with the B1 on the 5.10pm York train. Unfortunately it was often late running which caused problems of a different kind. The dilemma for us all was whether to hang on that little bit longer and risk the wrath of respective mothers who always had tea on the table at 6pm. Happy days. **c.1953 ● ARTHUR BENDELL**

Moston Station lay in a shallow, and reputedly dreary cutting which is seen to good effect when viewed from the west side of the line, north of Moston Junction signalbox. At this point the embankment bordered on fields behind Moston Mill, whilst over the line a footpath hugged the perimeter fence from Nuthurst Road to Moston Station. An equally dreary unkempt loco, ex-LMS 0-8-0 No **49508** trundles its train through the station before entering Moston Exchange Sidings. The trio of Chadderton cooling towers and council built property dominate the background whilst a Manchester Corporation bus crosses Hollinwood Avenue probably working a 65 service (or perhaps an AVRO's extra!) **c.1955 ● J. DAVENPORT**

Metro-Cammell/Crossley bodied Leyland Titan TD5 No 3370
(GNA 409) stands at Nuthurst Road before returning to High Street.
This chassis and body combination resulted in a peculiar cab design.
On 14th July 1941 the forerunner of Service No 212, route No 32 was
further extended to terminate here having already been extended from
Upper Conran Street to the Ben Brierley earlier that year. A triangular
island lay at the junction of Moston Lane and Nuthurst Road and
offered a convenient turning facility. By the time of the photograph, the
service had once again been extended to the Gardener's Arms although
certain extras, such as this, only went as far as the triangle. The open
expanse of Broadhurst playing field lies behind the pre-war vehicle.

c.1954 ● R. MACK

A **Bolton Class Five, No 45290,** bursts out dramatically from
under Nuthurst Road Bridge with an eastbound train of rail and
engineer's spares bound for Castleton Long Welded Rail Depot.
As well as dealing with a short block section of the Calder Valley
main line, (Colliery Junction and Vitriol Works Signalboxes were
both only 1 mile distant), Moston Junction Signal box controlled a
great volume of freight routed through the northern end of Moston
Exchange Sidings. These may be glimpsed through the first arch.
After passing the photographer, the train is now within sight of
Moston Station but will first pass under a 'pipe bridge'. This, part
of the Thirlmere aqueduct, carries drinking water from the Lake
District to the Manchester area, having flowed at the leisurely pace
of 2 miles per hour for all of 106 miles - destination Audenshaw
Reservoir. Work on the system started back in March 1890 yet
was only completed in 1968, the final year of steam on BR.

1966 ● BERNARD CRICK

NUTHURST ROAD

The rural character of Moston has been preserved over the years through the generosity of one man, Sir Edward Tootal Broadhurst, who
made a gift of some 80 acres of land in 1919 as a thank-offering for the victory of the Allies. He wished that the property be specifically
earmarked for recreational purposes and that covenants would protect its future usage. A Rebuilt Patriot 4-6-0, No 45534 was named in his
honour but the loco worked largely away from the city, being based at Edge Hill, Liverpool throughout the 1950's. A local landmark overlooking both the park and playing field was Broadhurst Café, standing at the junction of Lightbowne and Nuthurst Roads. It was formerly
Alberti's Café, named after the Italian owner who had also built the property. Queens Road bus routes No 54 (Stevenson Square - Middleton)
and No 7 (Mandley Park - Brookdale Park) crossed here and during the 1950's, drivers of the latter service would often make unscheduled
stops enabling the conductor to replenish the billy can with tea (by prior arrangement with Joe). Bunting and Union Jack adorn the building
at the time of the Coronation celebrations.   1953 ● A. HAYNES COLLECTION

**Newly delivered to Rochdale Road
Garage in 1956,** Leyland Titan PD2/12
No **3424** (PND 424) was one of a batch
of 60 buses built with Metro-Cammell
'Orion' bodywork. Nearly half of them (28)
were allocated to the former trolleybus
garage to work as replacements for those
vehicles. It is seen here passing Nuthurst
Road on Moston Lane whilst working
Service No 80, Moston, Gardener's Arms -
Chorlton (Hardy Lane), a route shared with
Princess Road Garage who tended to utilise
their Daimler CVG6 models. Moston Mill
and chimney are visible beyond the semi-
detached houses.

1956 ● A. HAYNES COLLECTION

MOSTON STATION

Looking towards Middleton Junction from the Up platform. The original bridge carrying Broad Lane is evident whilst a gents' urinal can be seen under the bridge. A signal box was once situated on this platform at the south end but closed upon the opening of Moston Exchange Sidings and the Junction signalbox prior to the First World War. Note the boarded crossing, again under the bridge, offering passengers access to the Down platform. **1909 ● JOHN G. HARTSHORNE COLLECTION**

The widening of Broad Lane bridge in 1930 resulted in the compulsory purchase of surrounding land. Local landowner Tommy Hughes advertised additional plots whilst engaged in transactions with the L&YR company. Gone are the toilets and boarded crossing The incline leading directly on to the Down platform from the re-named Hollinwood Avenue is prominent. The bridge was both widened and strengthened with raised parapets to withstand the rigors of transformers being moved by road from the nearby Ferranti factory in Hollinwood. By this time the Permanent Way had also been considerably upgraded. **1929 ● JOHN G. HARTSHORNE COLLECTION**

Up Platform By Night

Only the streaks of light created by the headlamps and a long time exposure, betray the presence of a Stanier 8F 2-8-0 passing through the station with an eastbound freight. The buildings were built by the LMS to a standard design offering much improved passenger facilities. Ladies' and gents' toilets were provided together with a waiting room and enclosed booking hall. Sliding doors allowed access on to the Up platform whilst on the other side, one was situated at the top of an inclined path leading directly on to the Down platform. These doors remained locked when the station was closed and on more than one occasion, passengers were forced to climb fences and clamber down embankments when the staff failed to arrive for work! The information board urges people to 'Keep Britain Tidy' - a topical campaign which, one might argue, had little or no effect. The door to the Booking Office is evident, next to which was a small store containing a coke fired boiler providing for the central heating system. The waiting room radiators offered a welcome respite in the severe winters of the 1950's and 1960's for Manchester bound commuters. Ronnie Young was Station Master here for many years.   **1964 ● BERNARD CRICK**

L&Y Dreadnought 4-6-0 No 10418 passes through the station and beneath the three arches over which passed Hollinwood Avenue, with a Manchester to Leeds and Bradford train. Note the sign advertising land to be sold in conjunction with the widening of the bridge. Whether the small print was for the benefit of the passenger remains a mystery.   **1930 ● JOHN G. HARTSHORNE COLLECTION**

L&Y 'Highflyer' 4-4-2 No 1407 appears to have plenty of coal left in her tender after having worked through on a York to Manchester express passenger train. The loco, in fine condition, spent her early years working out of Leeds depot and will soon pass through Moston Station having just gone under the occupation bridge serving Mough Lane farm.

1912 ● JOHN G. HARTSHORNE COLLECTION

L&Y 0-8-0 No 1553 passes Mough Lane Farm with special coal requisitioned by the Navy. During World War One such trains originated from far and wide and were known as 'Jellicoe Specials', so named after the Admiral of the Fleet. The destination was either Wick or Thurso (further bound for Scapa Flow). The loco probably worked as far as York before handing over to one of North Eastern origin. From here the journey would continue up the East Coast Main Line and on to Scottish metals for the last leg. The disc carrying a black and white cross alongside the headlamp and attached to a bracket on the smokebox door was perculiar to the L&Y system. It denoted 'Right Of Way Goods', giving such trains preference over other traffic, including local passenger workings. Popularly known as 'Teddy Bears', the locos were built with large boilers & superheaters resulting in a slightly unbalanced appearance. No 1553, was introduced in February 1913, becoming LMS No 12847 at the Grouping. She was an early casualty within a class which numbered 80 members, being withdrawn in August 1931. A handful survived Nationalisation, the last to go being No 52857 from Wigan (L&Y) Depot in December 1951. **1916** ● **A. HAYNES COLLECTION**

The same location records Agecroft 'Peacock' 4-4-0 No **981** bringing a local Oldham to Manchester Victoria (via the Werneth Incline) commuter train towards the city. This was an unusual working for an Agecroft loco, and she may well have been borrowed by the parent depot, Newton Heath, who were occasionally hard pressed for motive power to cover the intensive suburban services.

1910 ● JOHN G. HARTSHORNE COLLECTION

MOSTON GARDENER'S ARMS

No fewer than six buses have gathered outside Chain Bar awaiting their return journeys. The nearest is a Daimler CVG6 on service No 113 to Sale Moor (North Parade), whilst behind is a Leyland PD2/12 working a 26 back to Cannon Street. The distinctive Gardener's Arms, a Boddingtons public house, was built in the early 1930's replacing licensed premises of the same name further down Broad Lane. Apparently a drink called 'Jimmy Wilde' could only be obtained in the sawdust (vault) there.

c.1960 ● A. HAYNES COLLECTION

BUS SERVICES TERMINATING AT MOSTON GARDENER'S ARMS IN 1960:

No	Route	Garage
26	Cannon Street - Waterloo Road - Cheetham Hill - Crumpsall - Blackley - Moston	QR
65	Trafford Park - Stretford Road - Piccadilly - Oldham Road - New Moston	PR & RR
80	Chorlton - Alexandra Road - Piccadilly - Oldham Road - Moston	PR & RR
112	Sale Moor (Helsby Road) - Stretford - Piccadilly - Rochdale Road - Conran Street - Moston	PR & RR
113	Sale Moor (North Parade) - Stretford - Piccadilly - Rochdale Road - Conran Street - Moston	PR & RR
D	Rhodes Bank (Oldham) - Greengate	O

BUS SERVICES PASSING MOSTON GARDENER'S ARMS IN 1960:

No	Route	Garage
54	Stevenson Square - Oldham Road - Lightbowne Road - Middleton Junction - Middleton	QR
56	Cheetham Hill - Bank House Estate - Hollinwood Station	QR

Garages: QR - Queens Road   PR - Princess Road   RR - Rochdale Road   O - Oldham (Wallshaw Street)

Oldham Corporation Leyland No 202 stands in splendid isolation on Hollinwood Avenue at the Greengate terminus awaiting return to Rhodes Bank on the 'D' service. A sizeable number of the Corporation's fleet, resplendent in their crimson and cream livery, assembled here during rush hour on weekdays during the 1940's/50's serving the nearby AVRO factory. Vehicles frequently queued from the Gardener's Arms roundabout to Moston Station! They were all designated as 'D' service but would display various destinations within the Borough on the blinds. A combination of car ownership and a streamlining of the work-force brought about the curtailment of certain services and from the mid-1960's they were able to share the private bus station on Greengate. This had previously been the domain of Manchester Corporation's vehicles but by now AVRO's had passed into the hands of Hawker Siddeley Aviation.

c.1953 ● A. HAYNES COLLECTION

Leyland PD1/1 No 3038 (GVR 240) stands under the wires at a deserted Gardener's Arms prior to working a Sunday trolleybus service to Church Street. During the period leading up to the abandonment of the trolleybuses in the Moston area, motorbuses would often substitute or share the duties.

MARCH 1955 ● R. MACK

On 25th April 1955 the service converted to motorbus operation. The No 212 Gardener's Arms to Church Street linked up with the No 49 service which had operated between Manchester Piccadilly and Sale Moor. The newly created cross-city services were the Nos 112/3 which ran from Moston Gardener's Arms to Sale Moor (Helsby Road) and Sale Moor (North Parade) respectively. This brought Princess Road's Daimler CVG6's to the north of the city - all 90 examples of this class were based at the Moss Side garage. No **4166** (KND 927) swings round the traffic island before commencing the first stage of the journey into the City Centre. The route via Moston Lane, Upper and Lower Conran Street and Rochdale Road remained the same as its predecessor. The CWS sports ground stands over the island at the corner of Victoria Avenue East and Greengate (behind the bus). It is currently the home of North Manchester Rugby Union Football Club.

JULY 1960 ● R. MACK

The last trolleybus left the terminus, without ceremony, on 7th August 1955. Another cross-city service was created in the form of the No 80 to Chorlton, (Hardy Lane). Leyland Titan PD2/3 No **3270** (JND 671) stands by the timeclock before leaving with the twenty minute interval service, which was shared between Princess Road and Rochdale Road Garages. One year after inauguration, alternate buses (re-numbered No 88) ran to White Moss, leaving Moston Lane by the Fourways Cinema, travelling down Charlestown Road to Booth Hall Road.

AUGUST 1957 ● J. FOZARD

A. V. Roe and Company was formed in 1910 by Alliot Verdon Roe, a Mancunian who had become the first Englishman to fly a powered aircraft during the previous year. AVRO's premises were originally in Ancoats, followed by Newton Heath before moving to much larger, purpose built premises in Chadderton in March 1939. The vast majority of the workforce transferred there and large numbers of buses were necessary to cater for their transportation. A private bus station accommodating up to 70 vehicles was provided on the west side of Greengate immediately opposite the factory.

The trolleybus service No 32 from Church Street to Moston Gardener's Arms was extended to AVRO's bus station on 23rd August 1943 for certain rush hour journeys only. Ten years later the service was renumbered 212. The driver of Crossley No **1176** is on the front upper deck from where access was gained to the route indicators. With the assistance of the conductor's hand signals he is re-setting the blinds for the inward journey. No 1176 was the last member of a class of 40 ordered in March 1939. Divided between Hyde Road and Rochdale Road Garages, they possessed TDD4 chassis with Metro-Cammell/Crossley streamline bodywork. This example was withdrawn in May 1959.

c.1956 ● **D. YOUNG COLLECTION**

An interesting variety of buses are beginning to assemble prior to 'knocking off' time at 5pm. They were predominantly supplied by Queens Road and Rochdale Road Garages and tended to be the older vehicles still in capital stock. Hyde Road also regularly supplied Crossleys for journeys to and from the eastern suburbs. The towns of Hyde, Denton and Reddish, all via Belle Vue, were each catered for by two or more vehicles. No **2917** awaits departure at 5.10pm on Service No 106X to Denton. Service 136X was extended to Glossop and this was often in the hands of the unique Crossley, No 2937 - the only member of the class fitted with platform doors. The bus stops here are of interest, being a selection of original tram stops deemed surplus to requirements by the Corporation Transport Department. c.1953 ● **K. WALKER COLLECTION**

CHADDERTON POWER STATION

Vitriol Works box stands immediately behind ex-LMS 0-8-0 No **49557**. The area beyond was known locally as 'Slack Valley', as was the original Power Station, although the works which once occupied the site was owned by Hannibal Becker & Co. The word 'Vitriol' translated means 'acid' and a number of chemical plants in the area supplied products used in association with the abundant cotton textile industry. The Power Station, which possessed its own locomotives, developed facilities and sidings which were extended in 1952, necessitating a new signalbox. The new architect-designed BR Type 14 version, complete with flat roof, replaced a smaller ex-L&Y structure of the same name in 1954. It contained 65 levers and had a standard LM frame.

c.1955 ● J. DAVENPORT

Andrew Barclay 0-4-0ST Chadderton No 2 was delivered new on 23rd June 1955. She carried a dark blue livery, lined in white.
29th JUNE 1955 ● HAROLD D. BOWTELL

The locomotive eleven years later, by which time she was austere and unkempt. The distinctive earlier livery is now but a memory.
7th MAY 1966 ● R.S. GREENWOOD

Passenger services between Manchester Victoria and York via the Calder Valley were largely in the hands of Agecroft and York locos. Newton Heath, however, was responsible for a handful of duties including this, the SSO *(Summer Saturdays Only)* 1.40pm Liverpool Exchange to Bradford express which offered a connection with the morning boat from Douglas, Isle of Man. The immaculate seven coach set of vermilion and cream stock is roofboarded but the point to point timings were woefully slow. The train was booked to stand in Victoria from 2.38pm to 2.50pm! Hughes 'Crab' 2-6-0 No **42708** is ideal motive power for such a job and is seen here ambling past Vitriol Works on the approach to Middleton Junction.
15th AUGUST 1953 ● ARTHUR BENDELL

The 10.10am York - Manchester Victoria and the 5.10pm return had been a Sheffield Millhouses Jubilee duty for many years, prior to which Compound 4-4-0's Nos 1198/9 had been regular performers - supplemented by 2P 4-4-0's Nos 563/4. Millhouses took delivery of a new batch of Standard Class Fives (Nos 73013-16) in September 1951 and they were used on the service for a short period. The ex-LNER depot at York then took over and supplied Thompson Class B1 4-6-0's until the end of steam working on the service. No **61176,** which with No 61224 had arrived from Darlington earlier in the month to supplement the York stud, is approaching Middleton Junction with the evening train. With a wisp of steam from her safety valves, the evening sun captures much detail whilst the driver has noticed photographer Arthur Bendell recording the scene. His train is passing at between 35 - 40mph on the steady climb to Rochdale - its first stop.

23rd JULY 1953 ● **ARTHUR BENDELL**

LMS 0-8-0 No 9546 rattles its train of vans along, leaving Middleton Junction in the distance and is about to pass Vitriol Works Signalbox on the way to Moston Exchange Sidings. This example was withdrawn shortly afterwards, in September 1949. **c.1948** ● **J. DAVENPORT**

Agecroft Class Five No 44782 passes through Middleton Junction with the 2.02pm York to Liverpool Exchange. Reporting Number C234 was allocated to this train which comprises a motley collection of Gresley stock, preceded by a parcels van of possibly North Eastern origin. This loco and sister No 44781 were both kept in immaculate condition at the Salford depot and were often employed on this train. Part of the Agecroft diagram involved the 10.15am Manchester Victoria to York, then the 2.02pm throughout to Liverpool Exchange followed by the 6.30pm return to York which the loco worked as far as Wakefield.

c.1956 ● J. DAVENPORT

One of Newton Heath's long serving tank engines, Stanier Class 4MT 2-6-4 No **42623**, gets away from Middleton Junction and returns to the city with one of the many Rochdale to Manchester Victoria local trains.

c.1956 ● J. DAVENPORT

The 'Andy Capp' engine. A certain notoriety is attached to ex-LMS Compound 4-4-0 No **41101**. She was selected to haul a special excursion from Manchester Victoria to Blackpool in July 1959, organised in conjunction with the Daily Mirror, for which purpose she adopted the rather garish livery of yellow and black (applied at Gorton Works). No 41101 had been much travelled, working out of Wigan (L&Y), Walton, Bolton, Southport, Bank Hall, Blackpool and Lancaster during the 1950's. She is pictured approaching Middleton Junction with a Liverpool to Rochdale slow.

c.1952 ● ARTHUR BENDELL

Evidence of new BR ownership is apparent on the tender of Lanky 'A' Class 0-6-0 No **52137**. This lightweight train approaching Middleton Junction is more than likely the Saturday 5.35pm Manchester Victoria - Todmorden early evening service, which was a Newton Heath duty. During the week the train was in the hands of a Llandudno Junction or Holyhead loco on a filling-in turn. The last three coaches are of the ex-Midland Railway close-coupled variety. The occupation bridge in the background was one of two between here and Moston station which were demolished in the early 1950's.   JUNE 1952 ● J. DAVENPORT

The 6.03pm ex-Victoria to Middleton rolls into Middleton Junction Station behind Fowler Class 3 2-6-2T No **40015**. The Up platform holds a Stanier Class 4 2-6-4T ready to leave under clear signals with a local from the Castleton direction. Rarely did one observe three trains together here, but the coaches occupying the Werneth Branch Down form the 6.52pm to Rochdale via Oldham.   **11th JUNE 1951** ● H.C. CASSERLEY

Ex-L&Y 2-4-2T No 50850 is about to depart from the Oldham platform with an enthusiasts' special organised by the RCTS. After crossing Rochdale Canal and passing Chadderton Junction, the attack on the notorious 1 in 27 Werneth Incline will start in earnest. The train has rear end assistance in the form of Lanky 'A' Class No 52271, a type well versed in this kind of work. The check rail indicates the severity of the curve here and the peculiar contour of the timber platform on the Up line, together with the fencing, create something of a ramshackle appearance.

17th SEPTEMBER 1960 ● G. HARROP

Traffic heading north up the Calder Valley was faced with a continual climb through the northern suburbs of Manchester. The double track Middleton Branch converges at the platform end beyond which were Up and Down running loops extending to Mills Hill Bridge, some half mile distant. Firwood Cotton Mill and chimney are visible to the right of Middleton Junction North signal box and this was one of a cluster of such mills in the immediate vicinity of the station. The private sidings of the CWS Preserve Works lay beyond the Up loop (behind the box) and offered alternative local employment, as did the popular John Willie Lees 'Greengate' Brewery. **8th MARCH 1964 ● G. HARROP**

MIDDLETON STATION

The view looking east away from the platforms shortly after closure to passengers. Upon departure, Manchester bound trains were immediately faced with a short gradient of 1 in 80/86. As well as a two-platform station, other facilities at Middleton included a goods yard on the Down side, whilst mineral traffic was catered for behind the station buildings on the Up side. In common with many other signal boxes, the locking room windows had been bricked up amidst a general air of neglect and desolation. The poster sited in the box above the nameboard reads 'Wilful Damage' etc, perhaps as a result of recent theft or vandalism. Ironically the Middleton Branch had suffered many years earlier at the hands of Sinn Fein extremists who severed telegraph wires in June 1921 during a one-night campaign around the Manchester area. Shunters' cabins are prominent and beyond them a home signal protects the Branch from the throat of the mineral yard. Part of the Dane Mills complex stands aside the loading gauge and was rail connected from the goods yard.　　　**11th SEPTEMBER 1964** ● **G. HARROP**

The austere and rugged appearance of a 'Breadvan' was somehow in keeping with that of the surroundings here. Fowler Class 3 2-6-2T No **40015** is up against the stop blocks, having arrived with the 5.12pm from Manchester Victoria. Many would consider this duty just about within the loco's capabilities - they were decidedly unpopular with footplatemen! A spartan service of six trains in each direction after the war survived until the bitter end, which came on 4th September 1964. By this time steam had given way to Diesel Multiple Units which still transferred to the Up platform for the return journey, in keeping with the old L&Y practice. Sunday services had been withdrawn during the First World War and, for reasons of economy, were never re-instated. Goods traffic lingered on for a further twelve months before final closure, which came about on 11th October 1965.　　　**11th JUNE 1951** ● **H.C. CASSERLEY**

The Middleton Central Gardens, which opened in October 1934, were always considered to be a colourful asset to the town, being well tended to by the local Council. They lay in the fork formed by the Manchester Old and New Roads in the town centre and from here a variety of buses both stopped and terminated. A local service, No 121, was introduced between Wood Street and Middleton in November 1954 but was extended in March 1956 to run from Bowness Road to Church Street, Manchester - at which time it became the first Langley 'limited stop' bus. In April 1957, the old 61X, running between Bowness Road and Manchester Piccadilly during rush hour only, became the 122 (the 61X having also been introduced in November 1954). On 27th January 1969 - shortly after the end of steam - Service No 121 was converted to 'Pay-as-you-enter' and further extended to Manchester Chorlton Street Bus Station. This conversion was in common with other routes at this time.

A quartet of buses are held in rush hour traffic on Manchester New Road alongside Middleton Gardens. The leading three are all Leyland PD1/3's of which No **3053** carries a deep white band above the driver's cab. This signified to the observer, a Queens Road allocated vehicle but the treatment was only applied to batch Nos. 3050-99, all of which were delivered new there in 1947/8. Another coincidence is the Mackeson advert with slogan variations consistent with the media campaign during that period.

c.1960 ● R.H.G. SIMPSON

MIDDLETON CENTRAL GARDENS

Leyland PD2/3 No 3291 stands on the west side of the gardens whilst passengers board for their city bound journey. Note the floral tubs over the pre-cast concrete bus shelter. Service No 59, running from Shaw, Wren's Nest to Cannon Street, was jointly operated between Manchester and Oldham Corporations and tickets overprinted with the word 'joint' were issued between Chadderton and Middleton only. On this occasion however, the bus may well be starting out from Mills Hill Bridge with a shortened 59X service. Also prominent is The Middleton & Tonge Co-operative Societies' Departmental Store on Manchester Old Road which was a popular outlet for all manner of household goods on the north side of the city.

c.1960 ● R.H.G. SIMPSON

MANCHESTER IN THE DAYS OF STEAM

FRONT COVER **A Stanier locomotive in all its glory.** One of the most successful and popular locomotives was undoubtedly the Jubilee Class 5XP 4-6-0. Introduced in 1934, the class numbering 191 examples, could be found all over the ex-LMS system and were the pride and joy of very many locomen at various depots. Farnley Junction shed (25G) had a small number on its allocation, primarily for working the Liverpool - Hull express passenger trains between Leeds City and Merseyside. Long-standing resident, No 45708 **Resolution** is about to attack Miles Platting Bank in earnest with the 9.30am from Liverpool Lime Street. Nos 45581 *Bihar and Orissa*, 45646 *Napier*, 45695 *Minotaur* and 45705 *Seahorse* were stablemates from October 1952 and these five shared the work with Edge Hill shed who provided locos for certain diagrams.

JUNE 1951 ● ARTHUR BENDELL

BACK COVER **LMS 2P** 4-4-0 No **40676**
Miles Platting Bank   1955 ● A. HAYNES

Manchester Corporation Crossley No **2020** (GVR 114)
Stevenson Square   1963 ● R. MACK

Austerity 2-8-0 No **90357**
Moston Exchange Sidings   1966 ● PAUL JORDAN

Jubilee 4-6-0 No **45635** *Tobago*
Manchester Victoria   1962 ● M.L. HARRISON

Stanier Class Five 4-6-0 No **45200**
Newton Heath Station   10th AUGUST 1958 ● P. HUTCHINSON

Stanier Tank 2-6-4 No **42624**
Failsworth Station   24th SEPTEMBER 1955 ● A.C. GILBERT

Steam
IMAGE